Alys Fowler

ABUNDANCE

HOW TO STORE AND PRESERVE YOUR GARDEN PRODUCE

PHOTOGRAPHS BY SIMON WHEELER

This book is dedicated
to those who taught me
how to make jam –
Dor Dor, Lizzy and Denise

CONTENTS

INTRODUCTION

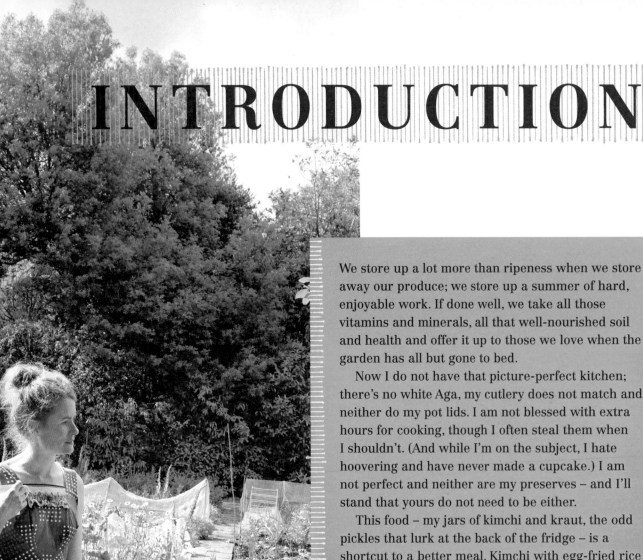

We store up a lot more than ripeness when we store away our produce; we store up a summer of hard, enjoyable work. If done well, we take all those vitamins and minerals, all that well-nourished soil and health and offer it up to those we love when the garden has all but gone to bed.

Now I do not have that picture-perfect kitchen; there's no white Aga, my cutlery does not match and neither do my pot lids. I am not blessed with extra hours for cooking, though I often steal them when I shouldn't. (And while I'm on the subject, I hate hoovering and have never made a cupcake.) I am not perfect and neither are my preserves – and I'll stand that yours do not need to be either.

This food – my jars of kimchi and kraut, the odd pickles that lurk at the back of the fridge – is a shortcut to a better meal. Kimchi with egg-fried rice or those cheap packet ramen noodles is not fine cuisine, but it sups and fills in a wholesome way, it stays seasonal without feeling impoverished, it is both a fulfilling and filling way to eat.

My cupboards lined with jars, the shelves burgeoning under their weight, amount to more than just food for the winter. They are a store of knowledge – like a library for my vegetables – they speak for the season behind me, another year measured in flavour and form. They are not only a reminder of what I have grown, they also satisfy a fundamental need to provide for myself in the leaner winter months.

There are well-versed statistics on how unsustainable our food production has become: 15 calories of energy are used for every one that is eaten; 20 per cent of global emissions are caused by processing, transport, packaging and retail of our food; waste of this food accounts for another 3 per cent, and land grabbing and deforestation for yet another 18 per cent. Put in this light, it's not travelling to New York for a weekend that's killing off our world, it's eating out-of-season food shipped from everywhere but here. Therefore, a viable local food system, one that won't account for almost half of our global emissions, needs commitment to seasonal eating – and this means preserving seasonal food for those months when we can't, and frankly shouldn't, have fresh aubergines or courgettes.

The potatoes in the cold store, the pumpkins resting in the hallway, the seeds saved for cooking, as well as growing, are all part of a vital cycle that makes it possible to live year round on what I grow. Yes, there are meals that are sparse on what many rely on as staples – that Mediterranean trio of tomatoes, aubergines and courgettes. True, by the end of the winter I long for buttery soft summer salads and sweet new potatoes, but I never feel deprived by my own or my garden's limits. I would be lying if I said that I didn't eat out-of-season food – that train sandwich, the fruit bowl at a conference. Sometimes it is good, but mostly it is a disappointment to my own precious food memories. I want to hold dear to an English summer strawberry wet from the rain, I do not need to fill its place with something too crisp and too bland (even if its colour and size are enticing).

As we rush forth our world is ever faster, yet more connected. I know I am not alone in wondering whether this is quite the hole I wish us to tumble down. I sometimes feel like I am clinging onto a root, shouting wildly down into this hole demanding whether anyone knows what skills we'll be needing down there in the future.

I love the collective nature of online life, I love the fact that I can tap into any one of you to help find the answer, but I believe that we are losing perspective on which skills actually matter. There is a huge difference between learning from a book or online to learning from a practitioner. It's a cliché, but so much of a skill can be lost in translation.

I still cannot bring myself to believe in a world where all the solutions to our mid-century traumas will come about through technological change. Call me a Luddite, but I am holding on tightly to my preserves and my good organic potatoes that store well because I believe that food is what will carry me through with grace and good economy – not how fast I can access my smartphone. So I am backing timeless knowledge that has been shared collectively, skills that have been truly used and most importantly practised and passed down. I am sorry if your grandparent is no longer around to teach you how to bottle, but please, before that cycle hits again, teach others what you learn.

While your grandparent would have been able to look over at your pot and say instantly, too thick, too thin, not enough acid, you need another ten minutes, I cannot stand there and shout 'not that way.' All I can do is guide you. You will make mistakes, things could explode, it might feel dangerous and downright dodgy. If so, please don't eat it. I know it took time and energy, but this, I'm afraid, is the downside of missing a generation of skill-sharing.

Your altitude, the temperature of your kitchen, even the size of your measuring spoon may affect the recipe. If you can get to a class on preserving, or adopt a grandparent to ask what is the best way through the sticky mess, then do. Be sensible, act cautiously, make small batches and vary them often – no one wants to eat the same thing for months – stick to timings, watch carefully and I can guarantee you will come away with something good to eat.

The history of preservation

It is said that early hunter-gatherers found the first dried fruits. This fruit would have dried in hot sands and winds. A sweet chewy fig or some dried berries, perfectly preserved by nature, must have seemed like a miraculous bounty. There is evidence from the Middle East that as early as 12,000 BC we had started to dry our own foods. The Romans positively loved dried fruit; there are numerous recipes, particularly for figs. The ease and simplicity of dried fruit makes it an obvious forerunner for our first forays into preservation.

It is lost in antiquity when fermenting arose, but it is most likely to have developed during the Bronze Age as a means to turn milk into yogurt and other sour drinks by the cattle farmers of the Indus Valley, now in Pakistan. There is a very whimsical story surrounding sauerkraut that a cabbage was discovered floating in the flotsam of the sea and it washed ashore as kraut (we do know that seawater was used in early fermentations). However, I think it is more likely that the Chinese invented a method for fermenting vegetables in rice wine around 3BC when the Great Wall of China was being built. It was said to have fed the army of builders and some accounts suggest Genghis Khan brought it to Europe. There are also accounts of Greek and Roman sauerkraut-like products fermented in wine and fruit juice. As unlikely as it may seem, one of the oldest continually cultivated vegetables is the cucumber. Originating from India, we know that it has been pickled for as long as it has been grown.

All of these methods of preservation arose for one reason – to feed us in leaner months. The early hunter-gatherers constantly had to be on the move so as not to overforage a particular area. Early preservation allowed us to stay put and sheltered or move further on to new territory if necessary; it offered up a degree of freedom.

We have learnt to salt, dry, ferment, sugar, boil and freeze our way to a better diet. Preserving food has allowed us to do all manner of things – conquer new countries (you cannot get very far on a long journey without some form of preserved food), go to war, create empires and dynasties, or climb into inhospitable areas and come back again to tell tales. We have built cultures and societies on a taste for certain foods. Wherever you go in the world, there is always some unique fermented product or a particular way of drying or salting. This aspect of cooking has allowed us to evolve from living by the laws of nature to dictating the rules. Without preservation, our history would look very different.

The commercialisation of preservation

The Industrial Revolution's technological progress was more than just coal and steam; it brought forth new diets through methods of preservation. The use of sugar, heat and packaging meant that we were no longer beholden to the fluctuation of the harvest. For the first time in our food history, mass production was possible. The taste and nutritional value of pre-industrial food was dire; the high mortality rate in young children was partly due to inadequate and unhygienic food. Food was poorly prepared and often deliberately adulterated – for the consumer, eating could be a deadly experience.

It was a vicious circle: the low nutritional value meant poor productivity at work, which meant less to eat.

All those 18th-century factories needed fuel, and one of the most far-reaching changes in our diet was the introduction of the South American genus, the potato. It spread from Spain, through to the Netherlands and fairly rapidly into Germany and Austria, making its mark throughout the rest of Europe. The potato can feed more people on less acreage than any grain; it thrives in damp cool climates and perhaps more importantly makes the cheapest spirit going, vodka. Although initially viewed with suspicion, once tasted, the potato rose in popularity to become one of the mainstays of the 18th-century diet.

At the same time, Germany provided the first cheap source of sugar. Until the 1800s, the only sweetener available was extraordinarily expensive tropical cane sugar, brought over by the Crusaders in the late Middle Ages, or the equally expensive honey. Although cane sugar production appears in Sicily and Madeira from the 15th century onwards, it remained a luxury for only the wealthiest. German beet sugar, however, was a different beast – easy to produce, cheap and widely available, it revolutionised preserving for the masses. For the first time you could take summer fruit and turn it into winter jam.

Potatoes, sugar, legislation against food adulteration (particularly for meat and flour), railway lines and steamships meant food could be distributed far and wide and with this you see a huge population boom. Our eating habits were changing rapidly, nations were being built on new foods and, for the first time in our history, Europe was pulling itself out of nature's grip. Famines were slowly becoming a thing of the past.

By the 19th century, urban areas were rapidly increasing and this again brought about more change in the way we ate. Food needed to be transported to the people and with transport came marketing and storage. Food packaging, and the marketing around it, began to make a huge mark on what we ate.

Whereas in the past, we had relied on salt, vinegar, animal fat (or olive oil in the Mediterranean) and alcohol or honey to keep the bacteria at bay, now we had the pressurised steamer (the ancestor of the pressure cooker). Using this it was possible to sterilise large quantities of food and seal the contents so they could last, if not indefinitely, at least through several seasons.

By the second half of the 20th century, eating habits were to radically shift again with the introduction of refrigerated and frozen foods. Preserving food with ice was nothing new. Since antiquity, frozen winter ice was used to store food, cool drinks and keep meat safe. Cutting nature's ice, block by block, was common right the way up to World War II. Root cellars and pantries were incredibly well designed and so efficient that early breakthroughs in artificial cooling were dismissed as expensive and unnecessary. Even my parents' generation remembers the pantry ruling over the fridge for efficiency.

Once electricity became common, fridges began to dominate the kitchen, followed quickly by freezers, which in turn gave rise to the supermarket. It seemed we had solved the age-old problem of hunger and storage. We had conquered nature.

Nutrients, nutrition and nature

This huge technological shift in how we process food has of course brought many benefits, but also many losses. Refrigerated trains, planes and trucks have driven us further and further away from seasonal shifts. Much has already been written about this and I am assuming you are here because you have already swung to the seasonal side.

I am not suggesting that we should throw out freezing or tin cans – they both have their uses – rather that we should pick the very finest methods of preservation that truly ennoble our food so that we can eat well out of season. Some of these techniques are ancient and some are relatively new, some your grandmother would have used, others are from different cultures, but all of them bring a certain kind of grace to the winter table.

About these recipes

There are elements of recipes in this book that must be stuck to. These bits I can claim no prize for; they are mostly timings, percentages, the precise bits that have been tested, codified, written down and passed on by several generations. These bits must remain the same: the ratio of salt or acid needed, the length of a rolling boil. They are here for your health. Mess around with them and you might just produce something that is truly deadly in the form of botulism. Bad bacteria move in quickly under the right conditions and thus it is paramount to keep your hands, utensils, jars and surfaces clean. This does not mean spraying the place from top to bottom with antibacterial products (you'll kill off a lot of good bacteria that way) – just use hot water and maybe some soap, but mostly very hot water.

If you feel that a jar went wrong, that you missed a step or your instinct tells you something is not quite what you expected, throw it away. Signs that the contents are not right are broken seals, dried foodstuff around the lid (the contents have leaked), unnatural odours or cotton-like mould growth (white, blue, black or green) on the food surface or underside of the lid. Low-acid foods, in particular – bottled tomatoes that have gone wrong – may contain botulism. Botulism can be picked up through the skin, as well as through digestion, so don rubber gloves, bag up your offending jar and throw it away. It is not safe to go on the compost. (Other jars that have gone mouldy – pickles,

chutneys and jam etc. – are perfectly safe to send through a bokashi or bio-digestor for compost, but may attract rats if you put them on a regular home compost.) Saying that, I've composted a lot of very wrong contents in my time and lived to tell the tale.

As long as you get your ratios right and stick to the cooking/waterbathing times, the rest is up to you. Feel free to add a little more chilli, a little less pepper and so on as you see fit. You own your kitchen, not me. Go forth and invent. What works for me may not work for you – that is the essence of good homecooking, it is adaptable. This is not cuisine; this is your garden and kitchen coming together to provide something every day of the year. And adapt you must, there should be no waste. Yesterday's vegetable ends are tomorrow's stock.

The lowdown on botulism

Botulism has killed the home preserver before – rare, yes, but very possible. It has definitely made many people very sick. The most likely place to pick up botulism is from waterbathing vegetables and fruit that are too low in acid. The classic examples are tomatoes and green beans. Tomatoes vary wildly in acidity, with different varieties or growing conditions and storage methods affecting their levels, which is why modern recipes for waterbathing always call for the addition of acid, usually in the form of lemon juice or citric acid. (The latter is more appropriate as it is measured acid, unlike lemon juice which can also vary in acidity levels.) The issue with clostridium botulism is that although the bacteria are killed off by high temperatures (hence the waterbath), it is very hard to kill off their spores, which can withstand much higher temperatures than boiling water. It also

happens to be able to thrive in anaerobic conditions inside the jar. Hence, although it may look dandy inside, the spores can still grow, producing a toxin that can cause botulism. Saying that, don't let this put you off. Botulism spores are found on most fresh food surfaces, it's only in the absence of air that they become dodgy. Follow these few simple steps and they will no longer pose a threat. Botulism spores are rendered useless and cannot survive in acid environments – that's anything below 4.6pH. Therefore make sure you always add enough acid to low-acid foods higher than 4.6pH. If you want to process low-acid foods, you will need a pressure canner – but I am afraid this book is not the place to learn about that. The USDA National Centre for Home Preservation is a great site, with all the latest scientific knowledge behind such things, so I'd start there.

ON GROWING

In *The Legendary Cuisine of Persia*, Margaret Shaida writes that in Iran a 'green-thumb' is believed to be 'the first necessity for making good pickles'. I take great heart in this belief because to me it makes sense. I can see that there is a strong affinity with good growing and good eating. And to put away good keepers for the winter requires a summer of studious growing.

Pests, diseases, a drought or floods, a little too much shade for sun-loving vegetables, a pumpkin that has rested too long on one side – all of these factors will affect the sum of the produce. Therefore, we must strive for the very best examples to go into store and enjoy the slightly dishevelled or marred ones on the day of picking – where with just a little judicious chopping they can be turned into something delicious.

If only growing the perfect vegetable could be captured in a chapter or explained in a few good paragraphs. Yet anyone who prides themselves on growing champion onions (to their table at least) or perfect peppers will tell you there is always a year that catches you out – there will always be a new pest or some crazed weather to vex you.

With every year I grow I have learnt that the best battle plan is not to go at gardening as if it is some objective science that can be broken down into factors or single threads, but to see it as a whole – a tapestry if you like – and to work on that picture.

ON SOIL

We are fed by our soil. Of course the plants and animals raised on it make for a better supper than a plate of dirt, but the truth is without good soil you have nothing to harvest. There are nuisances to a good harvest – disappointing varieties, rain, sun, heat and even who's picking – but if the soil isn't right in the first place the rest is just a dusting on the issue.

The route to the best soil is through compost. In short, the more organic matter you add the better your soil will become. It is that simple. Whether you have sandy soil, or poor urban rubble or clay, the remedy is always compost, preferably homemade. Good compost is magical stuff. In heavy soils, it binds to the clay allowing air and water to penetrate better. In sandy places, it bulks out the soil with organic matter, absorbing water and capturing nutrients. It does similar things to urban rubble. Most importantly, compost feeds the soil-food web – the little wriggly things you do not know the names of: the fleas, microbes, bacteria and fungi that make up the living architecture that is soil.

Worms and beetles, millipedes and nematodes all need food and at the very bottom of the chain is rotting organic matter. The more you make and add the better your soil will become. Manufactured fertilisers might seem like a convenient shortcut, but they are not the same thing as making your own. You could say it's much like the difference between a multi-vitamin pill and a good meal. You'd hardly expect a child to grow on vitamin pills alone and you shouldn't expect your soil to either. Many chemical fertilisers disrupt the soil-food web, microbes, bacteria and fungi become redundant and desert the soil, which is fine when the going is good, but not when things go wrong and you need them back. Pests, diseases, floods and drought are all warded off by healthy soil, which acts in defence of the plant.

Studies suggest that soils too rich in nitrogen can affect fruit quality and storage. Too much nitrogen can affect the plant's metabolic rate (essentially it grows too fast) and this ages the fruit faster. Conversely, an abundance of potash (potassium) in the soil has a positive effect on storage. Comfrey, seaweed, green manures, animal manures and rock dust are all beneficial because they add potassium into the soil.

ON COMPOST

Essentially what you are aiming for is healthy soil that produces unblemished, disease-free vegetables that are perfect for storing. One of the best ways of maintaining healthy soil is to mulch with well-made compost twice a year in spring and autumn (see page 27). Not only will this feed the soil-food web, but it also helps ward off diseases such as potato scab due to the balance of beneficial bacteria and fungi present. Thankfully, all the skill in making compost is down to harnessing nature's ability to rot stuff down. All you have to do is bring the right ingredients together in the first place.

Siting and building a compost bin

Firstly, you need somewhere to pile your ingredients up. This can be anywhere, but it makes sense that it is somewhere easy to access, but not in view. Compost piles are not the most aesthetically interesting focal points. Under a shady tree where little grows, behind the shed, tucked into a corner – just don't use up good growing space or site it in full sun.

What your bin is made of is entirely up to you. Mine are made from old wooden pallet boards, however I also own a worm bin and bokashi bins – both of which are ideal for smaller spaces – and a biodigestor (see page 24). I take this subject very seriously.

Wooden bins like mine, made from old pallet boards, are easy to construct and free to make. If you have enough space, position several bins together in a row so that you can easily turn one bin into the next, which allows you to make more compost, quicker (see page 23). Three bins is a perfect number. When constructing your bins, make sure you have easy access at the front to make turning and unloading your bins easy. How you strap your pallets together depends on your carpentry skills. I tend to use stakes rammed into the ground to keep the sides upright and sturdy.

Covering your bin

A cover is essential, especially on semi-rotting compost, to trap in heat. If you have any old carpet or rugs handy these make ideal covers because they allow rain to penetrate the compost (moisture is key) and offer good insulation to speed things up. To some extent, a cover will also keep out weed seeds that are floating around in the air. No one needs extra weed seeds!

Collecting rainwater

Compost can dry out quickly and if you allow this to happen you will end up destroying all the beneficial bacteria that are doing the hard work turning your waste into something good. I tend to keep a few buckets around my compost bins to collect rainwater (rainwater merely because it's free and easy to collect, but there's no harm in tap water). Drenching your compost with water also deters rats and mice that will happily move into your compost pile if it's nice and dry. A dry pile is like an invitation to a better life – free food, warmth and a perfect nesting place. A regular dousing of cold water is your reminder of who's in charge of the pile!

Tumbler bins

These are invaluable in small urban gardens, especially if you want to speed up the process of making compost. The idea here is that they allow you to regularly turn the compost, by spinning the bin. This method has many benefits – your compost is made super quick and it is vermin proof. The bin can be quite expensive and some people find they are difficult to spin once filled, but they work well for small quantities. For best results, it's worth having two bins to avoid adding new material to mostly rotted compost.

The ingredients

Everything, or at least everything that is natural, can be turned into compost. However, you might want to steer away from cooked food, dairy, pet poo (unless your pets are vegetarian), meat and fish – that is, unless you own a bokashi bin or biodigestor (see page 24). These ingredients will all attract rats and mice, who happily move in for free meals. Pet poo can also contain toxins which are bad for your health.

Everything else goes in – old cotton, wool or silk clothes, newspaper (scrunched up first), weeds, prunings, tea bags, vacuum bag waste, hair, toilet roll holders, vegetable peelings, grass clippings, cardboard, juice that's gone off in the fridge, pasta water, coffee grounds, shredded bills (no one is going to go through your compost for details of your bank account!), pet bedding and any packaging that is biodegradable.

There is lots written about how you have to layer up your compost – with a layer of brown and then green, and that certain patterns favour good compost – but in truth, this is all about speed. You can dump stuff in any which way you want, it just might take an awfully long time to get to compost.

To make compost fast you need a ratio of two-thirds carbon source – that is, newspaper, cardboard, old leaves, brown stems, prunings – to one-third nitrogen (greens, waste peelings, fresh weeds, grass clippings, etc). This golden ratio allows the bacteria to flourish. If you want your compost quick, and you do, try to make the layers no more than 15–20cm deep using different ingredients for each layer – that way, the bacteria will have a party.

Aerating your compost

Oxygen is an important part of the process, particularly if you want the bacteria to flourish, and one way of getting more oxygen into the compost is to turn it regularly. This is where having extra bins comes in; once the first one fills up, you can turn it into the next bin. How often you do this is partly determined by how quickly the bin fills up and how much you like turning compost. I hear that Prince Charles's bins get turned once a week; I turn mine once every three months or so.

Bokashi bins and biodigestors

If you want to compost meat, fish, dairy and cooked foods, I've found the best way is either to use a bokashi bin (can be used in conjunction with a worm bin) or a biodigestor (sold in the UK as a Green Cone). These systems use special bran that is inoculated with bacteria to quickly break down the cooked food into compost. Often, particularly with the bokashi bin, the food doesn't look decomposed one bit, but the bacteria has done its magic inside the waste. Essentially it is zombified and once dug into the ground or added to a worm bin it rapidly breaks down into organic matter. Supposedly you add the bokashi bin contents to your compost, but you'll need to bury it because if you leave it on top you will get an explosion of flies. I often bury my bokashi bin contents into the ground (see picture right). I find this is particularly good for bean trenches or enriching pockets of poor soil.

The biodigestor is an in-ground composter that is moved every five years. The waste is added to the cone and it rots away into the ground, so there is nothing to harvest. The great thing about a biodigestor is it can also take cat and dog poo. However, it is very important that you do not put anything with a carbon content, such as pet bedding or paper in as this will slow decomposition, allowing different bacteria to move which can make the process unsafe. I keep my biodigestor next to my apple trees, which thrive off all the good organic matter leaching into the soil. The worms also go bonkers for it.

Dealing with pernicious weeds

It is never a good idea to add pernicious weeds, such as bindweed, dock roots, couch grass and the like, directly into your compost. Unless your compost is very hot (around 50–60 °C), those beastly weeds will not be killed off (they are well adapted to not rotting down quickly) and when you spread out your compost, you will spread out all those weeds. Weeding them out the first time is a bore, a second time and you may lose the plot.

For small quantities of pernicious weeds, I tend to rot them down first in my buckets of water before adding them to the pile. Once there are no visible roots remaining, and the mixture has turned into a strong smelling weed soup, I simply throw the contents on top of the compost. All the good nutrients the weeds have been robbing from the garden are returned into the compost and the rats get a smelly wake-up call!

For larger quantities of pernicious weeds or truly infested clumps of soil, it's a good idea to double-bag them in waste bags and leave them to rot down fully before adding them to your compost; this can take up to three years so hide them somewhere out of sight and direct sunlight which will degrade the plastic bags. Once all sign of green life is gone, simply add them back into your compost heap – preferably in stages because the end product can be quite acidic and heavy.

The results

The results of your composting should smell good, clean, wholesome and earthy. A strong smell suggests your compost needs longer in the bin; the most likely cause is it is too wet, so add more cardboard, straw or newspaper and turn it regularly to aerate it. If you add in more layers of cardboard each time you turn, it will quickly turn into something good.

The finished product should feel damp and have the look of rich dark chocolate. How broken down the matter becomes is partly determined by what went in. If you included a lot of large prunings, cabbage stems (or other tough lignified material), it will take longer to break down (only fungal activity can go to work on lignin and that's a longer process).

To remove large pieces of bulky material, all you have to do is sift your compost before use. You can buy compost sieves, but I find an old metal shopping basket does the trick just as well. All that shaking is a proper workout, but you'll be rewarded with beautifully even compost at the end. Just don't forget to throw the large bulky stuff back into the compost bins for another round.

I spread my compost twice a year – once in early autumn and once again in spring.

Spreading your compost

Autumn is the perfect time to spread your good, well-rotted compost over any cleared beds. A good couple of inches is best. You do not need to dig it in; in fact, it is better that you don't. This mulch acts as a blanket, protecting the soil organisms below from the winter cold. Over autumn, the worms will work a fair bit of the new source of food into the ground, which will help to aerate the soil. All those worm tunnels, as they move the food from above ground to below, create channels that allow the winter rain to penetrate and move freely through the soil. Heavy soils such as clay accumulate a lot of winter rain and once it gets cold it freezes in the soil. These soils take a long time to heat up in spring, making early sowings problematic. The more compost you add, the more worms, so the less you have of this problem.

Worm tunnels are so well constructed they remind me of the large concrete culvert pipes laid under motorways for drainage. That is, until you take your fork or spade and break them up. Leave the worms and their tunnels alone and you will see remarkable results. Not only will you be rewarded with beautifully aerated soil, but you will also avoid disturbing the weed seeds, which means they won't germinate, so much less work for you!

Refilling your compost bin and covering it for winter

Now that you have finished mulching, and your first bin is empty, you can refill it with all the new material that you have accumulated at this time of year, including all the spoils of harvesting as you cut things back. There is no need to touch the middle bin; as long as the contents are turning considerably darker, there is no need to worry about this bin much. Your third bin should be in an almost finished state, so that it can sit over winter, gently rotting away, ready for the spring spread. The only thing left to do is to cover over the second and third bins to keep them warm and protect them from the worst of the weather. Winter rain can leech a lot of good stuff out of the compost and a cover will protect against this.

In spring, use the compost in much the same way as you did in autumn – to spread over any beds that are now empty of winter greens or to mulch around newly planted vegetables to keep weeds down and lock in moisture.

Making leaf mould

Leaf mould is not broken down in the same way as regular compost and needs to be treated differently. Making leaf mould is a slow process that relies on fungi and plenty of water and air, but if you have the patience you will be rewarded with some of the finest soil conditioning stuff out there, not to mention a great seed compost addition. The best thing to use for this is a chicken wire cage (a simply fashioned four-sided cage made out of chicken wire with stakes for each corner). If you do not have space in your garden for this, black bin bags punched with holes will work just as well. All you need to do is fill them up with your autumn leaves and walk away. In a year's time you will have wonderful, dark black 'gold' to spread on your garden or sift for seed compost. Leaf mould will reduce in size by one-third, so pile the leaves up high. What looks like a huge amount at the beginning will reduce to very little by the end.

ON SOWING

My neighbour's mother is Austrian and she was born in a small mountain town where her parents ran a guesthouse. She remembers how at harvest time the whole farm (for it provided not just for the family but for the guests as well) would get ready to put by. The cabbage would be shredded on great huge mandolins, the apples would be sliced into rings to dry in the attics, cider was made for all who needed sustenance, redcurrants were jammed, gherkins were pickled and herbs hung in the loft. She remembers how no one ever went hungry, not even during the war, such was the care taken to grow and store the harvest.

Today there is little obligation to preserve on this level, but even for the home-grower it is worth researching which varieties store well. As a rule of thumb, be wary of any variety that claims to ripen earlier and more uniformly than the rest. It is often only by days – a matter of great importance for commercial growers trying to pip their competition to the post on to the supermarket shelf, but of little relevance to you. Today everyone seems more obsessed with getting an earlier and earlier harvest, but home preservers thrive on staggered harvests with space to breathe between batches, not gluts when everything arrives at the same time.

Best keepers

When it comes to storing, not all the peas in the pod are alike. There are versions for shelling immediately to eat on a summer's evening and versions for storing – and that is true of most vegetables.

Last spring my allotment neighbour, Ann, gifted me a marrow that she has grown for decades exactly because it stores so well. As I write here in February, these marrows are still perfectly good, sitting pretty next to my boots in the hall. They have good, firm, but not too thick skins and roast perfectly.

Through trial and error, I have found that it is mostly the older varieties of vegetables – those bred when bottling and root cellars were a necessity – that make the best storers. Seed swapping, the Heritage Seed Library and other seed exchange sites on the web are a great source for long-forgotten good storers and local varieties. Ask around, particularly of those gardeners who seem to be eating well in the winter months. Here is a list of varieties that will serve you well until you find your own Ann's marrow:

Apples
There are hundreds of varieties to choose from, but these store particularly well: 'Ashmead's Kernal', 'Blenheim Orange', 'Kidd's Orange Red' and 'Fiesta' are all good eaters till around Jan/Feb. 'Sanspariel' will store till March. 'Bramley's Seedling', 'Anne Elizabeth' and 'Lane's Prince Albert' are cookers that will store till March.

Artichokes (globe)
'Green Globe' is prolific and tasty with tight large green heads. Supposedly hardier than other varieties. 'Imperial Star' is an improved variety, but has been selected to grow as an annual. 'Violetto' is a purple-headed variety (goes green when cooked).

Artichokes (Jerusalem)
'Fuseau' is a less noble variety making it easier to clean and cook with. However, if you select the smoothest tubers of the straight species *Helianthus tuberosus* to replant each year you will naturally breed a smoother tuber yourself.

Aubergines
'Money Maker' is suitable for a cool growing season and can be grown in a pot (but all aubergines do better with some form of cover in the UK). 'Ophelia' produces slightly smaller fruits, but both have good flavour.

Beans
Broad Bean 'The Sutton' and 'Green Windsor' both freeze well. 'Aquadulce Claudia' dries well. (Note: pick beans young if plant has suffered from chocolate spot – if you leave them on the plant the fungus will spread to the beans.)
Dwarf Bean 'Cannellino' has delicious creamy white beans that work wonderfully in stews.
Climbing Bean 'Barlotta Lingua di Fuoco' is a climbing bean with pretty red and purple striped pods and marbled seed. Can be eaten fresh or dried. 'Neckar' is one of the best for freezing.
Pea Bean (orca bean) If allowed to swell, these can be shelled and dried to give pretty dark maroon and white beans. Pods can be eaten fresh when young and flat.
Runner Beans These are heavy croppers with long thin, pale green pods, which are good young. If allowed to mature, beans can be dried for use in soups and stews. 'White Emergo', 'Czar' and 'White Lady' produce pure white beans, which look the most attractive when dried. Note that the dried beans of red varieties turn a rather unpleasant brown when cooked.

Beetroot
'Cylindra' has long red roots, stores well in cold store and can be harvested over long periods. 'Forono' has a wonderful flavour, long roots and is excellent in cold storage, as well as in pickles. A great favourite, but will bolt if sown too early. 'Golden Detroit' has yellow beets that are delicious roasted. Stores well in the ground (unless you have slugs) or in cold store.

Broccoli

Broccoli (calabrese) 'Fiesta' F1 produces huge domed heads. Once the main head is harvested, it produces lots of smaller side shoots from late summer to autumn. Freezes well.

Italian Broccoli 'Romanesco' has large lime green curds; will produce a number of side shoots. Works well in pickles and freezes well.

Purple Sprouting Broccoli Has many small purple florets in March when fresh vegetables are at their lowest. Not one for storage, but definitely worth growing. 'Redhead' has larger primary heads, along with good-sized secondary shoots; you should be able to pick for 8 weeks.

Brussels Sprouts

'Seven Hills' is one of the best varieties for standing over long periods. As it's an old variety, it tends to mature over a number of weeks – meaning no Brussels glut.

Flower Sprout 'Petit Posy' is a cross between a kale and a Brussels sprout. Stands well in the cold and, as the sprouts are loose, harvests over a very long period.

Cabbages

The weight and density of the head determines how long a cabbage will store. 'Holland Late Winter' is harvested from November to December. Produces very dense, beautiful white flesh that is good for kraut. 'Kilaton' F1 is a hybrid resistant to clubroot. Produces large, round, dense heads harvested in late October; good for kraut. 'January King' stands well in frosts. Makes a large head with crinkly, Savoy-style leaves when planted in fertile soil. Will store

for a week in cold storage (below 10°C). 'Asturian Tree Cabbage' is a perennial cabbage that will survive up to two years if you cut off the flowering spike. With just a little protection – fine mesh netting or a little fleece – it will come through the winter. Provides large cabbage leaves (harvested like kale) pretty much year round if you stagger sowings. 'Portuguese Cabbage' *(Couve Portuguesa or Couve Tronchuda)* is a large, loose-leafed cabbage that never forms a head and is picked like kale. It is a key ingredient in many Portuguese, Brazilian or Cuban soups. I've found it to be reliably biennial and, with a little luck, perennial (it seems to do better in the very cold winters). The leaves will store for several days in a fridge – longer in a humid cold store – and tend to taste better in the colder months than summer.

Carrots

'Autumn King' is an old variety that stores particularly well over winter. 'Chantenay' stores well as does 'Kingston' F1 and 'Bagnor' F1. Early Nantes' and 'Amsterdam Forcing' sown late in July stand well in free-draining soil if covered with straw for frost protection, or in sand in cold storage. Note: check regularly for carrot leaf miner, which will happily munch all winter long in stored carrots.

Cauliflowers

'Aalsmeer' and 'Prestige' both have impressive large white curds, but they are often late to mature (around May for me). Make sure the curds are covered in January or they will be hit by frosts. Both varieties freeze well. 'Clapton' is club-root resistant. Can be harvested in

autumn if sown in early spring under cover. 'Graffiti' has deep purple heads ready in autumn. Excellent in pickles due to the colour.

Celeriac

'Prinz' has a good flavour and seems to resist hollowness, which is a big plus. Will need fleece or straw covering if you want to keep it in the ground.

Chard

Swiss 'Fordhook Giant' is a large white variety that I find to be particularly hardy. 'Rainbow Chard' is pretty, but eat the red varieties up first as they are the least hardy.

Celery

'Celebrity' is a self-blanching type with ribbed stems. Although the stems are short, it has a very good flavour. 'Ivory Tower' is self-blanching with tall, smooth stalks and good flavour.

Leaf celery This may not have long smooth stalks, but it is reliable no matter how bad the winter is and well worth sowing. Leaves can be used to season soups and stews. 'Variegated Radicchio di Treviso Tardiva' is a late maturing green variety with red specks to the leaves. The hearts are a lovely pink and green. Fairly resistant to frost and can be harvested until February if sown in a warm October.

Opposite: top left Asturian Tree Cabbage, top right Artichoke 'Violetto', bottom left Broad Bean 'Aquadulce Claudia', bottom right Brussels sprouts 'Seven Hills'

Chillies

Varieties for freezing: large chillies with thick flesh, such as Habaneros, Rocotos, Pablanos (also known as Anchos), Anaheim, Padrons and Oxhorn 'Diablo' (Note: Pablanos should be roasted and skinned first.)

Varieties for drying: smaller chillies, such as Cayenne, Thai and Bird peppers. (Note: these can be ground afterwards and used in kimchi, see page 111.)

Varieties for pickling: Jalapeños.

Corn salad

'North Holland' has decent sized leaves and is frost resistant if covered with fleece.

Courgettes

In general, the stripy green varieties seem to store for the longest, probably because they tend to have thicker skins. 'Striato d'Italia' is a good productive variety.

Marrow 'Tiger Cross' F1 is resistant to cucumber mosaic virus and has been bred for the British climate. Produces nice striped green courgettes if picked young. If left to mature marrows offer incredibly long storage.

Cress

American Land Cress is one of the hardiest winter salads. If you are eating it raw, you should pick it very young otherwise it becomes quite tough. If this happens, use as you would watercress in cooking.

Cucumbers

'Paris Pickling' is an heirloom variety dating back to the 1800s. Makes the perfect gherkin, the best of the pickles (see page 118). If you forget to pick young, will also make a fine salad cucumber as long as you peel off the prickly skin. Never bitter and does well outside whatever the weather. 'Marketmore' is an old favourite for large dark green fruit. Resistant to cucumber mosaic virus and produces over a long period.

Fennel

'Finale' has good firm bulbs and is as bolt resistant as a fennel can be. 'Mantovano' is an Italian fennel for spring harvesting. It is bolt resistant, as long as you keep on top of the watering. Produces slightly flattened bulbs with a very good flavour.

Garlic

Hard-neck types The Canadian-bred 'Music' is not easy to get hold of, but I have never found a better garlic for storing. Easily lasts a year in storage (see page 43).

Soft-neck 'Cristo' is a great all-rounder with a good flavour. Suited to UK climates, it stores well in cool conditions.

Kale

Black Tuscan Kale 'Nero di Toscana' offers by far the best flavour. Survives cold winters as long as it is a decent size.

Russian Kale 'Ragged Jack' is perhaps the hardiest, but I don't think the flavour is that exciting. It definitely improves after a frost, when it sweetens, but the leaves can be tough. Good for bulking out stews and such.

Daubenton's Kale or 'Chou d'Aubenton' is a perennial kale that will live for at least five years. (You can propagate it by semi-ripe cuttings in August if it gets a little tired.) Tastes better than 'Ragged Jack', but not as good as Tuscan Kale – saying that, being perennial, it does offer year-round greens. Sweeter after a frost.

Kohl Rabi

'Superschmelz' is a bit of a beast that can grow to the size of a football (ask yourself if you want to eat a football-sized amount in one sitting before you let it grow that big). Doesn't split and is resistant to bolting.

Leeks

'Musselburgh' is a reliable old favourite for good reason; it isn't at all bothered by bad weather. 'Babington's Leek' (*Allium ampeloprasum var. babingtonii*) is a native perennial leek that is very useful for early spring/ late winter greens. It has thick stems, much like leeks, but with fewer white parts, and can be used as a substitute wherever you might need leeks. In late summer, some of the bulbs can be dug up much like garlic. Its perennial nature makes it invaluable as a low-maintenance food source.

Lettuces

These are mostly water so they will never store well. However, there are varieties that laugh in the face of bad weather and that's quite exciting. 'Winter Density', 'Valdor' and 'Rouge d'Hiver' are all solid winter lettuces that can make it through the worst weather providing you give them a little cover with a cloche or fleece.

'Hungarian Black' chillies and many varieties of garlic

Mustards

'Green in Snow' is one of the hardiest winter mustards. It kicks a punch with spicy leaves. 'Giant Red' and 'Green Wave' are both surprisingly hardy (and both hot in flavour). 'Green Frill' and 'Red Frill', with their fine filigree of leaves, will also tough it through bad weather – although they aren't quite so spicy as the other varieties.

Onions

'Autumn Gold' is one of the best varieties for storing, with good yields. Produces firm, golden brown onions that should, with luck (and regular checking), keep until March. 'Red Baron' is a standard red onion variety with high yields. For a red onion, it stores well. 'Garnet' is similar in size and yield. Both are ready in August.

Salad onion 'White Lisbon (Winter Hardy)' is a reliable, if slow-growing spring onion that is happy to sit all winter long. It's quite thin so not so suitable for kimchi and pickles. 'Shimonita' is my favourite spring onion for kimchi (see page 111). It's a typical Asian onion with fat, tubular leaves and a sweet, mild flavour. Will easily grow to the size of a leek.

Parsley

'Hamburg Parsley' is a good dual vegetable: use the tops for flavouring soups and stews as a parsley/celery substitute; roast the roots much like parsnips; or grate raw and add to remoulade, much like celeriac.

Parsnips

'Gladiator' is an F1 variety bred for the British climate and, most importantly, its resistance to canker. A good flavour, it sits well in the ground and is reliable. 'Tender and True' shows good canker resistance and sits well in the ground, but can become a bit of a monster.

Pears

Pears have frost- sensitive flowers so look for varieties that not only store well, but flower just that bit later to avoid this problem. 'Beurre Hardy' and 'Conference' both ripen around October to November. 'Glou Morceau' ripens in time for Christmas and has an exquisite flavour, but it needs a sheltered spot.

Peas

I must admit that I always consume all our peas before I can even think of the freezer, but 'Green Shaft', 'Senator', 'Waverex' and 'Telephone' are all considered consistently good at keeping their flavour the other side of frozen.

Plums

No plum stores particularly well unless processed, but 'Marjorie's Seedlings' is disease-resistant and doesn't ripen until September to October, extending the season from early ripening varieties, such as 'Opal' or 'Czar'.

Potatoes

In general, maincrops are the best for storage, although in the right conditions many will make it through the winter. **Sarpo family** ('Mira', 'Axona', 'Kifli' and 'Blue Danube'): these are by far the best potatoes for organic growers. They are blight resistant, drought tolerant and, if kept cool, will store for a year! 'Blue Danube' is the best roaster; 'Sarpo Mira' is a good all-rounder and nice baked. 'Pink Fir Apple' is a wonderful salad potato that stores well through winter. 'Charlotte' and 'Belle de Fontenany' (not an early, but actually a wonderful maincrop) both store well.

Radicchio

'Palla Rossa Marzatica' is a late-maturing red-ball type chicory that can be harvested from December to January. 'Rossa di Treviso' is a non-hearting variety with deep red leaves and white mid-ribs. Excellent for forcing, it turns the prettiest pink colour. Productive over a long period. 'Tardiva' is the latest to mature, meaning you can harvest in March.

Radishes

'Black Spanish Round' is by far the most hardy winter radish. It can be incredibly spicy, so by late winter I tend to use it in kimchi or stir-fries rather than eating it raw. It has a thick, rough black skin, which I think is best peeled if eaten raw, and white flesh. 'Minowase' is a good mouli variety for use up to December. It is a Japanese variety with pure white roots. 'Red Flesh' is a tricolour radish from Japan that also does well in cold weather. It has a red interior and is mild in taste.

Rhubarb

'Victoria' is a very reliable variety that can be rejuvenated by splitting every five years or so, although you can leave it alone and it will still crop reliably. Has greenish pink stalks. 'Champagne' is an earlier variety with beautiful scarlet stalks (that look quite something when forced). Susceptible to slug damage.

Salsify and Scorzonera

Salsify and Scorzonera have long, thin roots resembling parsnips. Often referred to as vegetable 'oysters', they have nice-tasting shoots harvested in spring. In order to get a decent harvest you really need to grow them in very sandy soil, otherwise the roots fork and they become fiddly to peel.

Spinach

In my experience, any large-leafed variety freezes well after being briefly blanched in boiling water (see page 185). I like 'Giant American' for its deep green leaves and 'Bella' as a winter hardy variety. I tend to grow spinach as autumn and spring crops.

Squashes

Butternut 'Sprinter' does well in northern climates and stores well. 'Crown Prince' and some of the newer improvements, including 'Autumn Crown', I think are the best kobocha pumpkins. They need to be cured to improve their flavour before storing (two weeks or so at 25°C, where the starch will convert to sugar and then at 10°C for a month where more carbohydrates will be produced). Its peak flavour is somewhere between 1.5 and 3 months after harvest (before this it may just taste watery). 'Marina di Chioggia'is an old Italian variety with deep yellow flesh and knobbly blue skin. Improves greatly in flavour when stored.

Strawberries

'Alice' is a mid-season variety; very sweet and juicy, cropping from June to July. If you only have space for one, I'd recommend this variety. 'Flamenco' is an everbearer variety that is good for small spaces. Everbearers crop little and often from May to November, with peak cropping in September. Good for extending the season and dries particularly well. 'Malwina' is a late season variety that ripens into August. The berries are very dark red with an intense flavour. 'Symphony' has been bred to be mildew resistant. The berries have uniform shape and good flavour.

Swede

'Marian' is a heavy cropping purple-topped variety resistant to mildew and clubroot. Harvest from October to January.

Sweetcorn

This is another vegetable that I have yet to keep past the boiling pot. 'Lark' is an F1 variety that has been bred for cooler climates and is early to mature. It can be grown with other varieties with no need for isolating. 'Swift' is another F1 bred for our climate. It produces plenty of cobs and is tasty and reliable.

Tomatillos

'Mexican Tomatillo/Green Tomatillo' is prolific and the most reliable for less sunny summers. Bottles and freezes well; ripe fruit can be kept in a cold store for a week or so. 'Violet Tomatillo' is pretty and slightly sweeter in flavour, but less likely to ripen in poor summers. **Ground husk tomatoes,** or ground cherry (a relative of tomatillo): these are sweeter and taste a little like pineapple. Ripen towards the end of the season and are used mainly in sweet dishes. Can be dried, bottled in syrup or frozen.

Tomatoes

'Ferline'is a beefsteak variety with some resistance to blight. It has large red fruit with a good flavour. Happy growing in a pot. 'Latah' is a super-early salad type that tolerates cool summers. A bush variety, which likes to sprawl, it is a nice-looking tomato with a lovely balance between acid and sweetness. Good raw or cooked. 'Losetto' is a cherry type that is useful for container growing (it has a low sprawling habit making it best suited to pots). Blight resistant and the small fruit dry exceptionally well. 'Matt's Wild Cherry' makes for wonderful oven-dried tomatoes. A tiny cherry tomato, it is perfect for drying whole. 'Oregon Spring' is a reliable early variety and the hardiest of the bush types – a godsend with our summers! Lovely flavour with medium-sized fruits. 'San Marzano' is the ultimate tomato for pasta and pizza, however in northern climates it really needs to be grown in a greenhouse.

Turnips

'Snowball' is, for me, a great turnip to eat small (golf-ball size). It is an early maturing variety best for spring and autumn sowings. 'Golden Ball' is a maincrop variety with creamy, yellow flesh. Stores particularly well. 'Purple Top Milan' has pretty tops blushed with purple. Flattish in shape, they are quick maturing and do well in northern areas.

ON HARVESTING

I learnt to pick apples at the Royal Horticultural Society's fruit orchards. I was actually taught how to pick fruit – it was a lesson and we were graded. Woe betide if you squeezed too hard, or knocked the delicate bloom of a desirable apple that was off to be shown. Mr Arbury would shake his head slowly and off you'd be sent to try again. Cherries are picked by their strigs (the stalk) and never by the fruit, apples are cupped from underneath and then gently pushed upwards – if they snap off they are ready, if not you move on to the next. These details are important: every nick and every bruise will do hidden damage that will shorten the shelf life.

The skin on your fruit and vegetables is the membrane that protects it and keeps it in tip-top condition. Even innocent acts like washing your vegetables before storing them can cause havoc, as it can abrade the surface. When handling produce, make sure you are as gentle as possible: apples bumped or dropped, or too firm a grip on a cabbage will cause physical stress that will in time cause decay. One rotten apple truly does spoil the barrel.

Harvesting notes

Apples should be picked by cupping your hand around the bottom of the apple and pushing upwards. If it's ready it will fall off, if it holds on, wait a bit as it's not quite there yet. A perfectly ripe apple will always come off with its stalk.

Aubergines are ready when they are smooth and shiny; I prefer mine small. The UK climate is not suitable for large fruit production; smaller fruit picked often will encourage a longer period of harvesting. Cut aubergines, since snapping them could cause the brittle branches to break.

Beans (Runners and French) – pick when they are pencil thickness, with a hint of a bean inside, but still crisp – snap them in half to check. Runner beans are sweetest around 15cm or so, anything more and they become stringy. Once your beans reach the top of their structure, nip out the growing tips to stop them from continuing to climb – this will mean a bean you can actually reach!

Beans (Broad) – pick when the pods are thumb thickness and the beans will be small and sweet and won't need their skins removing. For fava or dried beans, leave the pods on until they are fat and begin to rattle (but dry the beans indoors). Note: broad beans need to be peeled off the stem by pulling down gently; it is very easy to snap the stem, so offer support if necessary.

Beans (Borlotti) – pick the first lot when they are young, the size of French beans, and eat whole. This will encourage the plant to produce more beans, which should be left to mature. The beans are ready when they have visibly swelled inside and the pod begins to shrivel.

Beetroots – baby beets should be picked when then are 5cm in diameter. These will be sweet with little or no skin. If you are careful you should be able to thin out your baby beets, leaving some to grow larger – although no bigger than a tennis ball. In hot weather, keep your beets well watered or they will become woody.

Broccoli/Cauliflower should be harvested in the early morning, when the heads are tightly developed and full. A head that is expanding is about to flower and will become tough and woody. You can encourage a second flush of smaller side shoots by cutting the stem just below the head. Broccoli does not do well in hot weather when it can become distinctly cabbagy in flavour.

Cabbages should be plump and firm (except for loose-leaf varieties from Portugal that always look a bit shaggy). A cabbage that is about to bolt will loosen its leaves and start to elongate – these can be used for stocks; the tender tops make a good substitute for spring greens. If the season has left you a little short, it is wise to make the cabbage work just a bit harder before its tough stalk hits the compost. To encourage a new flush of baby leaves, cut the cabbage head so that you leave as much stalk as possible behind, and then slice into the top of the stalk about 1–2mm deep to form a cross. From each corner new baby leaves will sprout. These will only grow to 5cm or so, but they are perfect for adding to soups and stir-fries. If the weather is mild, you may even get several cuts before you uproot and plant a new crop.

Carrots can be eaten at any stage. The top of the root will go green if it is exposed to light (if you don't want this, cover the surface with potting compost as your carrots develop). Carrots that are allowed to become too large have a woody core and lose sweetness. However, it is possible to leave carrots in the soil for up to a year before harvesting. These 'vintage' carrots will need slow, gentle cooking to improve their texture. Unless grown in the loosest of potting soil, it is wise to use a fork to remove carrots from the ground or you'll snap a lot of them in half. Carrot tops can (if the apocalypse comes) replant to resprout for carrot greens that are edible and make an attractive garnish.

Cauliflower – see broccoli.

Celery (particularly self-blanching types) should be harvested between August and November (definitely before the first hard frost). Trench celery is hardier and can be harvested well into December if covered with plenty of straw and some plastic – you might find the stems curl under the straw and plastic, but the flavour will still be fantastic.

Chard leaves can be eaten at any stage. However, for the longest production the plant should be sturdy and only the outer leaves pulled (never cut or they will bleed, causing loss of moisture in hot weather). Always leave behind 4–6 leaves to ensure continual growth. A chard plant will happily overwinter and grow into spring in mild weather, however it will start to flower as soon as the weather warms up.

Chicory and radicchio tends to survive down to −3°C (depending on variety). However, if it is a hearted variety it will only tolerate light frosts. Hearted forms should be cut by the end of November and kept as cool as possible until needed. Those that have not hearted will survive with a little fleece right the way through the winter. The harvest will be small, though, and only suitable for winter salads rather than cooking.

Cucumbers should be harvested small, anywhere from 10–20cm long. Small cucumbers are sweetest and make a great snack. By continually harvesting the cucumbers when they are small, you will increase production. If you want to pickle lots of small cucumbers, you will need several plants to harvest across. Large cucumbers are often seedy and bitter and best avoided. Lemon cucumbers are ready when they are a pale yellow; once they are bright yellow they will be hollow and seedy.

Fennel should be cut when the base has begun to swell to somewhere

Opposite: top left Raddichio 'Palla Rossa', top right Swiss Chard 'Bright Lights', below 'Blue Danube' potatoes

between the size of a golf and a tennis ball. You can tell if the plant is about to bolt (and they are very prone to bolting in dry or unsettled weather) because the top of the bulb will begin to elongate. If this happens, harvest immediately because the base will no longer swell. The fern-like tops can be cut up and used in salads or as a garnish for fish. The elongated base and tougher stems should be used in the stockpot.

Garlic – see onions.

Kale leaves can be eaten at any stage. Kale is often sold at farmers' markets as an entire cut-off top, but it makes much more sense to harvest only several leaves at a time from near the base of each plant. You can harvest baby leaves for salads. For continual harvest, the plants must be sturdy and well established. If you cut off the top, and the plant is mature enough, it will resprout but you will have to wait weeks and weeks before you can harvest again. A better approach is to leave at least 6–8 inner crown leaves to regrow. The bottom leaves should be composted as soon as they look tatty, as these are always tough.

Leeks can be harvested as baby leeks when they are thumb thickness or so. These are incredibly sweet and tender and you can eat pretty much the whole thing. Older leeks can be picked up until they send up a flowering stalk. When the flower stalk appears you have the choice of experimenting with the leek bulb at the base, which can be cooked much like you would green garlic or bunching onions. It is important to keep leeks well watered and to avoid getting

soil down the shaft when weeding (or you'll end up with soil particles in your dinner). If you want long, tall, white shanks, you will have to earth up. Remember when cleaning leeks to cut the root off and wash them upside down (roots upwards), as this ensures that any soil washes out from inside the plant.

Lettuce should be picked early morning or late evening when it is cool. To extend the harvest you should remove the outer leaves, a couple from each plant, rather than cutting the plant whole; a lettuce with just the bottom leaves removed can crop for up to 12 weeks. To harvest as 'cut and come again', cut the leaves when they are 10–15cm high, leaving at least 4cm above soil level to resprout. Always water well after harvesting and give a weekly liquid feed to boost a second flush.

Onions and garlic should be picked once the tops start to yellow. It is not necessary to bend over the stalks of onions, despite many saying so, as this can affect their storage life. Onions and garlic should be dried somewhere warm and airy (preferably outside); under a porch is ideal, especially if rain is likely. It is a good idea to raise the bulbs off the ground on a frame of chicken wire or similar to improve air circulation and speed up drying. They are ready for storage when the skins, tops and roots are completely dry to the touch and papery. At this point, the roots and stems can be cut off and the skins cleaned up for storage.

Garlic can be harvested green or wet in May; at this point, the bulb will not have developed into cloves and it will have a mild nutty flavour. Steam or fry and serve whole. Garlic flowers can also be eaten; these are called scapes and should be harvested when the stem is soft and pliable, before the flowers open. Can be eaten raw in pesto or lightly fried. I consider them a true delicacy and grow many hard-neck types (that tend to flower more readily) just for this treat.

Peas – pick either early morning or late evening, if possible, for the crispest peas. You need to pick regularly, every other day if possible, to keep the harvest up. **Shelling peas** should be picked when you can gently feel the peas inside the pod. The pod should be bright green and shiny – any cracking or yellowing of the skin will mean the peas inside will be tough and starchy. **Snap peas** or **mangetout** should be picked when the pod happily snaps crisply in half.

Pears should be picked as they begin to soften and change colour. Harvest late pears by October and store somewhere cool and frost-free to continue to ripen.

Plums should be harvested when soft and ripe. Don't over-handle ripe plums as they bruise easily and will need processing quickly.

Pumpkins and squash need the sun to taste best. Once you have two or three immature but developing fruits, you should stop the plant by pinching out the growing tip. This will concentrate energy into creating good pumpkins and squashes. Towards the end of the season, around September, remove some of the leaves around the fruits so that they can absorb the sun. You should

also gently turn the pumpkins so that they don't always rest on the same side on the soil. If it is not possible to turn them, raise them off the ground using an upturned plate or straw (be wary of slugs if it's wet); this will encourage the skins to harden. Squirrels and rats are very tempted by soft pumpkin skins at this stage, so take precautions. On harvesting, the skins should be hard (so hard that they can not be pierced with a fingernail). Always cut the pumpkin off with its stalk and a little of the stem intact. Despite this looking like a perfect handle, you should never carry the fruit this way as the stalk is easily damaged and this could affect storage (rot will quickly set in here). Ideally, pumpkins should then be cured somewhere very warm and dry (20–25°C) for 10 days; this process concentrates the starches into sugar. After this it should be stored somewhere frost free at roughly 10°C.

Marrows should have a hard skin that you can gently knock – but rarely at the beginning of the season will it be hard enough to withstand piercing with your nail. Again, do not handle marrows by the stalk.

Radish (winter types): winter radishes, particularly mouli types, often suffer from slug damage in a wet winter. The black types of radish are fairly frost hardy, but the mouli types dislike frost. For this reason, I rarely store radishes in the ground. Instead I uproot them and replant them in sand and store in bins (see page 56), twisting off the leaves first (these can be blanched or used for winter salads). Here they will store for a couple of months.

Salad leaves and stir-fry greens can be picked from several centimetres high to 10–15cm. Thus, you can use the thinnings or harvest as 'cut and come again'. 'Cut and come again' should be cut when they are roughly 5–10cm tall, and then you should get at least one more flush of growth – although these will become increasingly bitter and tough. After each cut you should water well and fertilise (particularly if growing in a pot) with a liquid feed. Once lettuce leaves start to ooze a milk sap they will begin to taste increasingly bitter and they will soon shoot to the skies to flower. This is a defence mechanism against slugs.

Spicy leaves such as rocket and mustard will taste very strong in both dry and cold weather. Mustards, in particular, can become unbearably hot and tough and are only good for cooking with in winter. Mustard should not be cooked for more than 30 seconds or it will become bitter. A cloche, mini-greenhouse or unheated polytunnel will offer enough protection to keep the flavour mild.

Spinach needs cool weather to do best. It should be grown as a late spring or early autumn crop. In heat it will quickly bolt. Baby leaves can be harvested as 'cut and come again' when they are 5–10cm high; to get a reflush of growth, there must be at least 2–4cm left above soil level. Otherwise, harvest when there are 5 or 6 'true' leaves, removing the outer leaves. You can harvest for some time using this method – just remember to water if it is dry or they will quickly bolt. It is wise to harvest spinach regularly to keep production up.

Squashes – see pumpkins.

Sweetcorn should be picked when the tassels turn brown and bend over. Peel back the sheath to expose the corn and pierce with your thumbnails – if the juices run milky it is ready to harvest; if the juices run clear it is not yet ready; if there are no juices it will have passed the point of being good to eat and is only fit as chicken food. The old adage that you should have the pan on to boil before you pick your sweetcorn is true; many varieties will turn from sweet to starchy in less than 30 minutes as the sugars deteriorate.

Tomatoes should be picked when fully coloured (unless a striped variety). Irregular watering, whether that's you or the gods, will cause cracking and splitting of thin-skinned varieties. If this happens, pick when they are just starting to blush with colour and continue to ripen indoors (never store in the refrigerator as this affects the flavour). If at the end of the season you have whole trusses of unripened tomatoes, cut them off whole and bring them inside to ripen. Either hang upside down somewhere warm or put in a bag or drawer along with some ripe tomatoes or a banana to speed up colouration (these give off ethylene, which triggers ripening).

Turnips – you shouldn't count on spring turnips for winter cold storage; the flavour will be too strong. For autumn and winter use, sow from July to September. A turnip should never be bigger than the size of a golf ball for sweetness or perhaps as large as a tennis ball for storage (although even at this size the middle will go hollow over time). Anything larger will taste mustardy, bitter and make you wonder why you grew them in the first place. The tops of turnips are edible and the tender middles are quite divine as a spring green. You can even push the off-cuts into producing a few more: simply cut off the tops of any large turnips so that there are a couple of centimetres of turnip remaining at the sprout end and place them in a bucket of sand somewhere warm. They will reshoot and the tender greens can be blanched and eaten as spring greens. Note: if you find that your stored turnips have resprouted leaves, these can be saved for the pot rather than adding them to the pail.

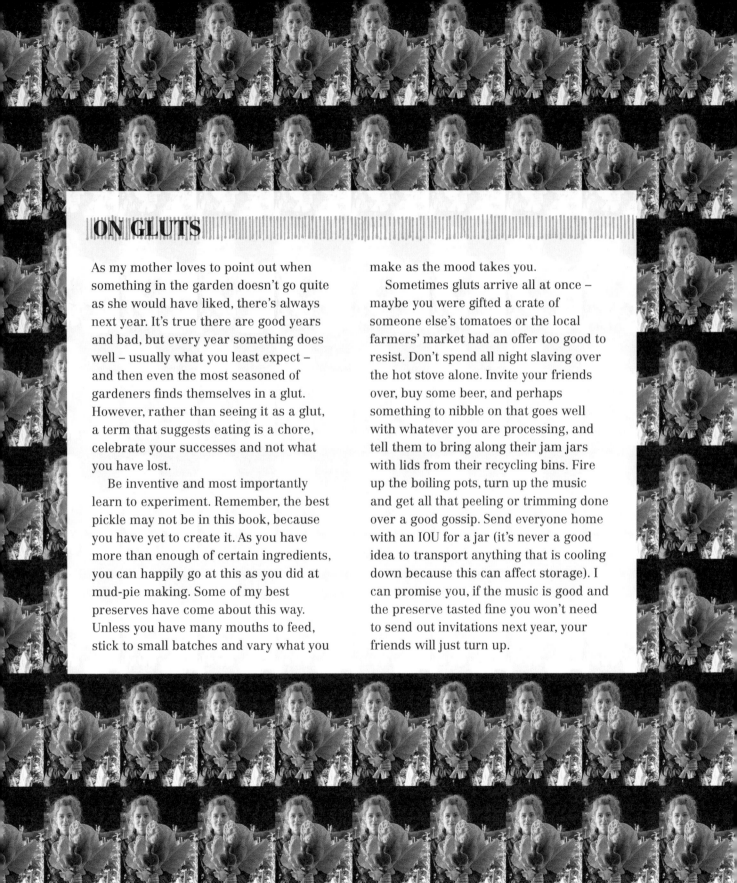

ON GLUTS

As my mother loves to point out when something in the garden doesn't go quite as she would have liked, there's always next year. It's true there are good years and bad, but every year something does well – usually what you least expect – and then even the most seasoned of gardeners finds themselves in a glut. However, rather than seeing it as a glut, a term that suggests eating is a chore, celebrate your successes and not what you have lost.

Be inventive and most importantly learn to experiment. Remember, the best pickle may not be in this book, because you have yet to create it. As you have more than enough of certain ingredients, you can happily go at this as you did at mud-pie making. Some of my best preserves have come about this way. Unless you have many mouths to feed, stick to small batches and vary what you make as the mood takes you.

Sometimes gluts arrive all at once – maybe you were gifted a crate of someone else's tomatoes or the local farmers' market had an offer too good to resist. Don't spend all night slaving over the hot stove alone. Invite your friends over, buy some beer, and perhaps something to nibble on that goes well with whatever you are processing, and tell them to bring along their jam jars with lids from their recycling bins. Fire up the boiling pots, turn up the music and get all that peeling or trimming done over a good gossip. Send everyone home with an IOU for a jar (it's never a good idea to transport anything that is cooling down because this can affect storage). I can promise you, if the music is good and the preserve tasted fine you won't need to send out invitations next year, your friends will just turn up.

ON STORAGE

By late August I can smell the apples ripening on my tree; likewise a strawberry at the right moment has a perfume so heady on a warm evening you can sniff out where it is. The slightly sour scent of milk that is turning, the ripening of bread mould, these are tangible signs that need no teaching other than trust. I know to trust my nose, to use my fingers to tell if the weight of a vegetable is right or rotten, to prod and pull to check what is right and what is wrong. Our senses are highly attuned to such things, though we have dampened these signifiers with best before and sell-by dates.

It is you, rather than any date, that can tell whether you should eat something or not. Trust your taste buds, if it fizzes or bubbles, smells odd, too sweet or too sour, then do not eat it. The only time you should not trust your nose or taste buds is if the seal on a waterbathed jar is broken (see bottling section). Here it is imperative that you do not taste the contents. Do not mourn the loss for it is your compost's gain. Nothing need be seen as wasted unless you wish it to.

To really know a vegetable or fruit, that is to understand its essential nature, means knowing it both in life and death and to take a great deal of notice of the moment that bridges these. This cannot be done at short notice; a season of growing will teach you a great deal, but several seasons later and you begin to understand how little of the surface you have scratched. The growing season is hugely important to storage, a wet season will turn soft fruit and vegetables quickly, a dry season may mean considerably smaller-sized produce that, in turn, dry out quicker. If you are to make it through all the seasons with food in storage you cannot take your eye off nature, otherwise your glib assessment will quickly be mocked. Observe your world carefully, with due care and you will dine well of it.

The shelf life of a vegetable, that is how long it can withstand without being anchored in the earth, has always been of great interest to us. Fortunes are made from getting peas picked, bagged and frozen in mere minutes or from rushing asparagus from Kenya to Kent, and we have to work hard to nurture plants that have a desirable shelf life. Of course, your shelves are a lot different to those of the supermarket. If, like me, you are city bound, you might not even have shelves. I certainly don't have a pantry; the storage space I have is nestled in the bathroom among the cleaning products, up in the attic among our forgotten things, by the front door next to our boots and in other temperature-dependent places. I make do and it gets us through. That's not to say I don't dream of a large pantry with cold slabs of slate and cool cupboards, but that is another life and until then I'm happy to adjust the one I have to house a few marrows here and there.

Indoor space is adaptable, but outdoor space needs to be a little more specific. Keeping the right vegetables in cold storage could mean you make it right the way through the winter with quite a considerable bounty – and if done carefully, it can be done for free (or very little) without the need for electricity.

Natural cold storage uses the earth as its freezer. Traditionally, this would have been a root cellar. Every house was once designed with special facilities for preserving food. An underground storage facility, whether it was a stone cellar or a pit, would have been part of the plan of a house. As I write, my knees bang up against a thick slab of slate that would have been my little house's humble version of this. My writing room was once the cold storage for this house. A thick slab runs right up into the brick wall, allowing it to draw cool temperatures from outside into the room. The floor is sunk into the ground and is merely covered with quarry tiles, so that it can draw up cool, but humid air. One day I hope to turn it back into a proper pantry, but until that time I shall write of such things.

HOW FRUIT AND VEG DECAY

Once the fruit or plant is picked, it starts the slow waltz to death. In a panic from the loss of water and nutrients, your bounty enters a macabre feeding frenzy and starts to consume itself, literally eating up its own sugars to keep breathing while accumulating waste products – that distinct smell of stored apples is this process in motion.

A few exceptions can hold off the battle – storage organs such as onions, potatoes and parsnips that have evolved to hibernate underground in cool temperatures, but the rest continue to dance to death's door. Your job is to freeze-frame this process, just long enough so that when you come to eat it your produce still tastes good.

The worst offenders, the ones that deteriorate more quickly, are the fragile vegetables such as peas, broccoli, corn and asparagus. With such thin skins, they panic immediately and rapidly convert sugars into starch, causing them to toughen up in their attempt to survive. This is why those frozen peas boast that they have been frozen within minutes of picking and taste so fine for it. They are still all sugar and little starch. This also explains the old adage for sweetcorn that says the pot should already be boiling as you begin picking.

Fruits are a little different – many improve with storage as they continue to ripen – but there is always a tipping point. Much like vegetables, once a fruit reaches the point of no return the only solution is to consume itself, not on purpose, but because the complex mechanisms that hold its life together fall apart and enzymes start random acts of destruction. The many microbes present in the air join in on the decomposition and before you know it there is compost in your storage bin (usually a reeking, rather wet version).

Stored fresh produce does best in a humid atmosphere. Fruit and vegetables are largely water and therefore don't like drying out. (Dry air will cause the cells to lose turgor and this, in turn, will damage the internal system.) Wrapping fruit in paper and storing root vegetables in sand or sawdust not only protects the outer membrane from damage but also stops your produce from drying out.

Although activity has rapidly slowed down now that these plants are not photosynthesising, they are still breathing, a lot. The excess carbon dioxide and water accumulate in condensation and this tends to collect on the food surfaces, which, in turn, encourages more microbial attacks. It is astonishing how much water accumulates. Open an unventilated bin of turnips and the lid will literally be dripping in perspiration.

Root cellars or cold rooms need to keep any

stored food at a low temperature and at the right humidity. Traditionally, this would have involved digging down into the ground to a depth of roughly 4 feet so that the stored vegetables were kept below the frost line. Here the earth naturally insulated the vegetables from truly cold temperatures because the soil below this depth was never expected to freeze.

On the ground where it is too stony or riddled with trees roots to dig down, storage rooms were built up using stones and turf to insulate them from winter cold and hot summers. These storage rooms were usually northfacing for obvious reasons. There are numerous designs for root cellars; the larger the room the more important it is to ventilate the space.

Vegetables in cold storage, although out of the earth, are not dead; they continue to breathe and release gasses, which if not properly ventilated for will build up and affect storage.

It would be very costly and inconvenient to try and build a cellar under an existing house and most urban dwellings do not have enough space for more ambitious cellars, but there are ways and means to make smaller, just as suitable storage spaces.

In-ground storage

Leaving your vegetables in the ground over winter is perhaps the simplest method of storage. You simply mulch on top with a thick layer of straw, dry leaves or other mulch and as long as it is done before the ground freezes your covered patch will remain easy to dig, even if the soil around it is rock solid. To protect your material from blowing away in winter storms, it is often necessary to cover the mulch to keep it in place. Heavier twigs or a sheet of plastic is ideal. The latter works well in wet weather because it keeps the row underneath dry, making digging much easier.

Raised beds, surprisingly, tend to freeze later than garden soil, partly due to the fact that there is often more organic matter incorporated in these beds so the soil is generally more friable and light. Here, a light mulching of straw or a little fleece over the vegetables may be all that is needed.

Although in-ground storage is certainly easier than lifting your veg and storing them somewhere else, it is not always ideal – and you will quickly learn how this sort of storage is an imperfect art. If you leave your vegetables in the ground, you run the risk of everyone else helping themselves. Squirrels made light work of my beets last year, despite the fact that I had left them tidily mulched, as did the mice and keel slugs who buried deep below, truly grateful for the winter snack I'd left.

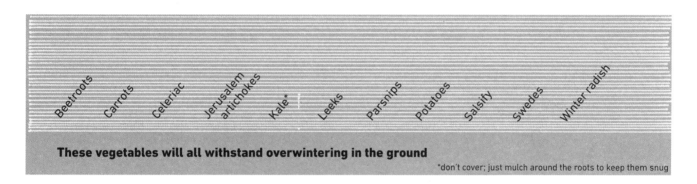

These vegetables will all withstand overwintering in the ground

Beetroots · Carrots · Celeriac · Jerusalem artichokes · Kale* · Leeks · Parsnips · Potatoes · Salsify · Swedes · Winter radish

*don't cover; just mulch around the roots to keep them snug

It is possible to dig up all of these and make a sort of shallow temporary pit, lined maybe with dried leaves or sand somewhere closer to the house or with easier access. Cover the vegetables with straw and, if necessary, shore up the side with old timber. You could create a lid with a piece of wood or just cover with soil and then perhaps a sheet of plastic to keep things dry and more soil to keep the plastic in place, or if it's a temporary store because you will use the vegetables up quickly, just cover with soil. This also makes land available to sow winter cover crops, such as green manures.

Some vegetables, such as carrots, parsnips and swedes, are all sweetened by the bite of the winter frost; the cold weather converts much of the starch to sugar, improving the flavour. If a bad frost is coming, a simple plastic cloche, a little fleece and other meshes will keep the covered vegetables a degree or so warmer. In truth, I dig up pretty much all apart from Jerusalem artichokes and parsnips, which I leave covered in straw and leaves. I find that in a mild winter the slugs often damage the rest to the point where there is little edible and in a hard winter too many are lost to frost burn.

But I can only keep emphasising how much of an imperfect art this is. Each individual growing space will have its frost pockets and warm corners. What you learn in year one of storage will only improve year two, three and the rest. There are no hard and fast rules here.

CREATING AN IN-GROUND COLD STORE

This traditional method, which was popular during World War II, involves mounding up your vegetables in a pile above the ground and covering them over with layers of soil and straw. While it could be said that an old-fashioned clamp is a thing of wonder, let me say here from bitter experience that making one truly is an art form – and to just blunder into mound building will leave you with mouldy potatoes! The key to success is ventilation and this would have traditionally involved fashioning a ventilation shaft from straw for the middle, and then covering the whole thing with up to 10cm of soil. I have made several over the years and although they have been fun to build, I do think there are easier methods. If you are hell-bent on clamping, I suggest you consult a pre-war gardening book and take note of the small details, especially on ventilation (stored vegetables tend to heat up initially in storage as more starches are turned to sugar so introducing fresh air is a must).

The modern equivalent of clamping is not nearly as pretty or romantic, but it works incredibly well and is a good form of upcyling. I have used this method successfully for a number of years. You bury a rubbish bin, either plastic or metal (although plastic is slightly better insulated). The joy of using a bin is it is cheap and completely watertight, as well as being vermin and insect proof. Several bins will hold the majority of your cold storage vegetables throughout the winter months.

Start by digging a hole at least 1.2 metres deep to accommodate your bin. If possible, you should keep the bin lid above ground in case of flooding. (If you want it lower than ground level, you will have to dig your pit considerably deeper and then line the base and sides with stones and rocks to create a drainage channel so that surface water is directed away from the bin.)

A little ingenuity is needed if you do not want to spend all winter lying on your stomach reaching into the bottom of the bin! I use florist's buckets and open mesh sacks to store my produce, both of which make for easy removal. Otherwise you could position the bin at a 45° angle to the ground (this method works well if you have to dig into a hill).

You can improve the insulation of the bin by storing your produce in sand, sawdust, dried leaves or straw. I prefer sand, as it seems to dissuade any errant slugs from taking up residence. It is very important that your vegetables and apples remain in a humid condition somewhere between 80 and 90 per cent relative humidity. Your vegetables' natural respiration will quickly moisten the environment and the sand will absorb this, whereas sawdust and straw can start rotting if the temperature rises, and this doesn't help things much.

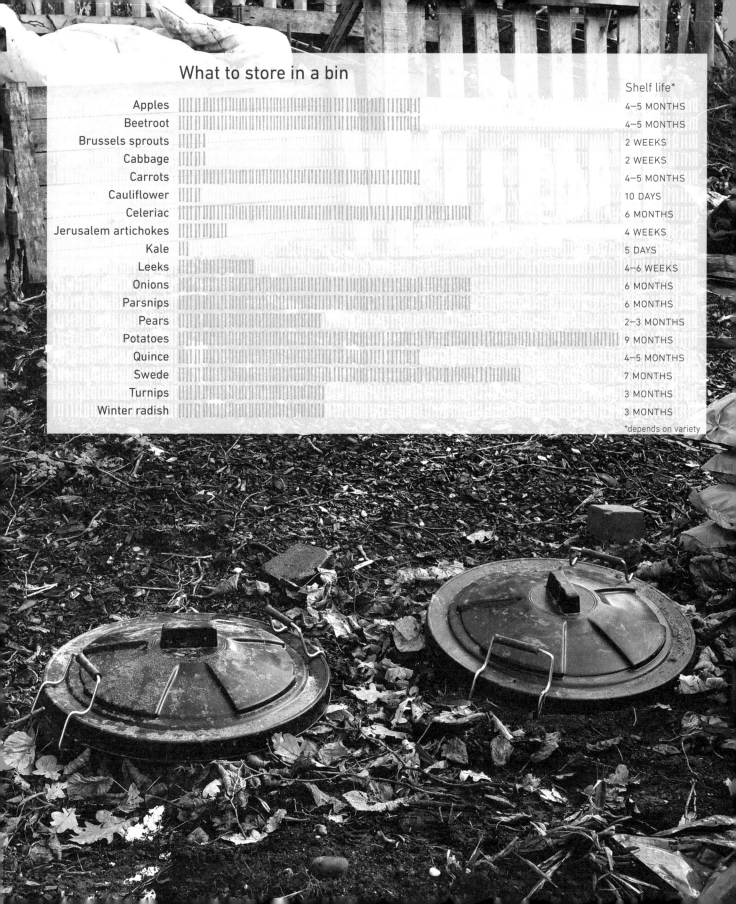

What to store in a bin

	Shelf life*
Apples	4–5 MONTHS
Beetroot	4–5 MONTHS
Brussels sprouts	2 WEEKS
Cabbage	2 WEEKS
Carrots	4–5 MONTHS
Cauliflower	10 DAYS
Celeriac	6 MONTHS
Jerusalem artichokes	4 WEEKS
Kale	5 DAYS
Leeks	4–6 WEEKS
Onions	6 MONTHS
Parsnips	6 MONTHS
Pears	2–3 MONTHS
Potatoes	9 MONTHS
Quince	4–5 MONTHS
Swede	7 MONTHS
Turnips	3 MONTHS
Winter radish	3 MONTHS

*depends on variety

What to store in your house (10–20°C)

	Shelf life*
Winter squash/pumpkin	6–7 MONTHS AT 16–20°C
Marrows	4 MONTHS AT 10–16°C
Garlic	5 MONTHS ABOVE 15°C
Onions	5–7 MONTHS ABOVE 15 °C

*depends on variety

Short-term summer storage

Terracotta pot fridges are widely used in Africa as a low-cost solution to refrigeration. The 'fridge' works by drawing up water from a saucer placed underneath, which soaks through the terracotta pots and keeps the contents cool. Strangely, this method only works in warm temperatures so you will need to keep your 'fridge' in the sun.

This method works especially well for tropical and subtropical fruit, such as aubergines, tomatoes, cucumbers, peppers and beans, which keep better at 10°C then they do in a conventional fridge, which is a bit too cold. (Under lower temperatures the cells of these vegetables begin to malfunction, causing enzyme action that destroys the flavour – if you don't believe me, leave a tomato in the fridge overnight and do a taste-test against a vine-ripened one the next day; the difference will be quite something.)

You will need two terracotta pots, one 8cm smaller in diameter than the other; a saucer; some sand and a lid. Place the small pot inside the larger one and fill the space in between with damp sand. Place on a saucer filled with water and top up regularly so that the sand remains damp rather than sopping wet. Fill the inside with your fruit or veg and cover with a lid.

ON DRYING

Something happens when you slowly dry fruit under the gentlest of heat – the very essence of the fruit is emboldened. Some fruits become better, more intense versions of themselves: sliced strawberries, for example, have so much more, well strawberriness when dried; other fruits take on new properties: a dried pear is chewy, sweet and almost fudgelike in texture. The idea of drying is not to desiccate the produce into something hard and parched, but to slowly release the water to leave behind a fruit that in midwinter is a treat rather than a chore to eat.

Drying, as its name suggests, works by reducing the amount of water in a fruit's cells. The natural water content of a plant (that you might want to eat) is somewhere around 90–95 per cent. When that number is lowered to anywhere between 5 and 35 per cent, the fruit is considered dried; in this state, many of the spoilage microbes can no longer survive and, hey presto, it's preserved.

What is suitable for drying?

Although it is possible to dry all manner of things from the garden, the truth is this is a process best used for fruit and perhaps seeds. Vegetables tend to lose their flavour when dried; they also lose a great deal of their vitamin content, the exceptions being tomatoes and chillies (which are both technically classified as fruit in the first place). However fruits, partly because of the natural acids, tend to hold on to their vitamins when dried. That is, if you dry correctly. Drying should be a slow process under very gentle heat to conserve all that is good. Even a hot radiator can be too quick and extreme.

How to make a screen dehydrator
You can fashion together a very simple screen dehydrator. Either use old linen pillowcases or go to a craft shop and buy some needlepoint canvas (the plastic stuff is good as it is rigid). If you are using cotton or linen then you will need to create a frame – use bamboo or sticks. The easiest way to do this is to turn up the ends with a needle and cotton so that you can thread the stick in to make a frame. Next you need to decide where you are going to dry – fairly high over the radiator is ideal. Otherwise, you'll need to fashion a stand and you may need to make several layers. Or you could just go on eBay and search for herb-drying rack and see what's on offer.

How to dry

In a hot country, you can utilise the heat of the sun to dry your produce – either by drying directly outside, traditionally using hot sands to bury the food, or by using a solar dehydrator. In wet, cold northern climates, however, we need to rely on artificial heat. While it is possible to dry fruit on a warm radiator, above a wood-burning stove or in a conventional oven (with a low temperature), my preferred method is to use an electric dehydrator. This has many advantages: it is efficient, being very low wattage; it can be on a very low heat setting, guaranteeing excellent results; and it enables me to dry large quantities at once. It is clearly not free, but it's a good compromise.

I have included an easy-to-make screen dehydrator that makes use of the house heat. It is ideal for drying herbs, seeds and smaller fruits. And you can place it wherever you can capture some heat: outside in the summer, in a greenhouse or porch, near a heat source (it works well in an airing cupboard).

You can dry apples on a pole hung above a radiator or oven. You will need to remove the core using a corer; it's up to you whether you want to leave the skin on or not. Rub the pole with a little oil so that the fruit doesn't stick and leave a couple of centimetres between each slice as when they dry they can bend and stick to their neighbour. You can also thread various fruits and mushrooms to hang to dry: you need a strong, thick thread, butcher's twine or strong string. Either thread or tie the fruit up and hang as necklaces over the heat source. I have also read about using a thorny branch such as sloe bush to pin the fruit upon and then hang this above a heat source, which seems a very natural and ingenious method.

Drying on the plant

The rattle of a runner bean pod at the end of the season is a sure sign that the beans are dry and ready for storing. For many seeds, drying on the plant is desirable; it is part of the natural cycle and means that the plant can transfer as many of the nutrients as possible to the seed, for it is in the plant's best interests that the next generation gets off to a good start.

Broad beans, runner beans, French and soya beans can all, in a good season, be dried on the plant. A wet autumn may thwart this venture, however, and then it will be necessary to bring your pods inside to finish the process in the warm. All you need to do is shell the beans and spread them out on a baking tray to dry. There is no need to apply direct heat; just place the baking tray somewhere warm (18°C is ideal) out of direct sunlight. The length of time they will take to dry will depend on the size and variety of bean, but I find a couple of days is usually enough.

While many people simply pour their dried beans straight into a storage jar after drying, it makes sense to sterilise them first to kill off any insect eggs. The best way to do this is to place the beans in a Tupperware container or similar and transfer them to the freezer for 48 hours. Make sure you remove them from the container before defrosting them or they will go mouldy; spread them out on a baking sheet or rack until they are fully dry and then pack them into airtight containers. They should keep for at least a year.

Drying seeds and herbs

Seeds such as dill, caraway and fennel are best collected straight off the plant early on a sunny day before the pods ripen fully and burst open. The best method of collecting the seeds is to place a paper bag over the seedhead and snip off the stem with scissors. If you bring the bag indoors and hang the seedhead upside down, gravity should do the rest. However, if the seeds are stubborn and not quite ready you may need to run your fingers over the seedhead to disperse them. If you end up with lots of chaff, tip the whole lot into a kitchen sieve and rub the seeds and chaff with your fingers to separate them. If they need further separating, you will have to winnow. On a breezy day pour the seeds from one bowl to another slowly, the chaff will blow away and the seeds will remain. If there's no wind, then you're going to have to blow.

A fine net or cloth bag, hung from the washing line on a warm, sunny day is useful for drying herbs such as marjoram or mint and other light material such as lavender flowers or rose petals. The advantage of a cloth bag is it will preserve the colour of the herbs, which would naturally bleach if left out on the plant in the sun, and it protects them from insects and birds. As long as you toss the contents regularly and bring it indoors at night (precipitation will dampen the bag and its contents), this is a simple and free way to dry things.

Drying fruit

All fruit benefits from soaking in a weak solution of acid to kill off undesirable bacteria before drying. This should also help prevent discolouration and, in the case of thicker-skinned fruit such as plums and grapes, softens the skins so they dry more quickly. You can choose not to do this, if you wish, but you will find that your fruit loses its natural colour and turns brown due to oxidation; this enzymatic browning can also lead to some loss of vitamins.

I use citric acid, but you could use lemon juice (in equal parts with water). Dilute 1 teaspoon citric acid in 1 litre water, put in your fruit and set aside to soak for approx. 10 minutes. If necessary, you can put several batches through the same solution.

The optimum temperature for drying fruit is 60°C. But you can dry at much lower temperatures. I dry apple rings in my kitchen near the radiator. Otherwise you can put the fruit on a tray in the oven on its lowest setting, use a dehydrator or try the airing cupboard.

Drying times vary considerably, depending on the age and size of the fruit and how it is prepared, with old fruit generally drying quicker than fresh fruit. Like many forms of preservation, the key to success is experimentation! To check if your fruit is ready, squeeze it between your fingers; it should feel pliable and leathery, with no moisture being released. If you are using a dehydrator, allow your fruit to cool before testing because warm fruit will always feel more soft and pliable (it will crisp up considerably as it cools). If you find your first batch of fruit is too dry, either shorten the drying time next time round or cut the fruit into thicker pieces. Common sense is key.

Before storing your dried fruit, it always makes sense to sterilise it first – especially if it has been dried out in the open where there is a risk of fruit flies landing on it. To do this, loosely pack your dried produce in a Tupperware box or similar and place it in the freezer for 48 hours. Do not leave the fruit in the container to defrost, or it will sweat and spoil; spread it out on a baking tray to dry fully and then store. Most dried fruit lasts up to a year, but starts to taste a little stale after that.

STEWED WINTER FRUITS

I think this recipe might be Polish in origin. I used to eat it at my friend Anna's house as a teenager.

> 2–3 large handfuls of mixed dried fruits
>   – apples, pears, dried plums,
>   strawberries and elderberries, etc.
> 1 Lapsang Souchong teabag
> 100ml warm water
> juice of 1 orange (optional)
> 2 tablespoons brown sugar
> a few cloves or some herb Bennet roots
> 1 small cinnamon stick
> a dash of sweet wine or damson gin

Place all the ingredients in a bowl and set aside to steep for an hour or so to allow the fruit to soften; remove the teabag. Cover with clingfilm and store in the fridge for a week or so. Serve with yogurt or cream or use as a topping for muesli or porridge.

How to dry fruit

APPLES: core and cut into rings 1-2cm thick – it's up to you whether to peel or not. Soak in citric acid or lemon juice for 30 minutes (see opposite) and then thread on to a greased pole, allowing 2cm between each slice to prevent them sticking together (they will curl as they dry). At 60°C they will dry in 8 hours; room temperature may take several days. Once dry, store in an airtight container somewhere cool and use within a year.

PEARS: peel, cut in half, remove the cores and cut into slices 1–2cm thick. Soak in citric acid or lemon juice for 30 minutes (see opposite) and then spread out on a tray to dry. For best results dry at 70°C for 8 hours. Store in an airtight container somewhere cool and use within a year.

RASPBERRIES, blueberries, bilberries, honey berries, elderberries etc: these are best dried whole. Soak in citric acid or lemon juice for 15 minutes (any longer and they start to fall apart – see opposite) and then spread out on a tray, making sure they don't touch. For best results, dry at 40°C; drying times vary, depending on size, from 7 hours. Store in an airtight container somewhere cool and use within 6 months. Makes an ideal topping for muesli and cereals.

STRAWBERRIES: cut into slices 1cm thick and arrange on a tray. For best results, dry at 40°C for 7 hours. Check regularly because you want them to stay bendy, rather than go brittle; note that strawberries lose their colour if they are overdried. Store in an airtight container somewhere cool and use within 6 months.

ELDERBERRIES are surprisingly sweet when dried and work well in muffins, cakes or savoury dishes such as tagines.

PLUMS: cut in half and remove the stones. Soak in citric acid or lemon juice for 30 minutes (see opposite). Arrange on a tray to dry, placing them skin-side down – this way, the centres will remain slightly sticky (this does hinder storage slightly, but improves taste). For best results, dry at 70°C for 10 hours. Store in an airtight container somewhere cool and use within a year.

Fruit leathers can be made from any fruit or fruit pulp, making this an excellent way of using up the leftover pulp from making fruit jelly (see page 136).

The process is very simple and involves pouring the pulp over a flat surface and leaving it to dry. The optimum drying temperature is 70°C. I find I get best results using a food dehydrator, but I have seen fruit leathers drying on top of wood-burning stoves and even on radiators before.

A good fruit leather should have a consistency of leather, supple and shiny. You can add sugar or not. If you are going down the sugar-free route, then I suggest mixing sweet fruit or honey to find the balance. Bananas (the older the better) and grapes are both good sweet bases to work from.

MAKING FRUIT LEATHER

You will need very ripe fruit; this is an excuse to use up all the just-about-to-go-over stuff – the sweeter the better.

> *Makes a 30 x 30cm piece*
> **200–300g fresh fruit of your choice**
>   **(the riper the better)** – *classics include*
>   *apple and raspberry, strawberry and*
>   *banana or just straight damson for a*
>   *delicious tart leather*
> **2 tablespoons lemon juice**
>   **(or ⅛ teaspoon citric acid)**
> **55g granulated sugar or 2 tablespoons**
>   **honey;** *honey is best done to taste*
>   *(optional)*
> **Flavouring of your choice** – *e.g.*
>   *⅛ teaspoon ground cinnamon,*
>   *cardamom, allspice, ginger or nutmeg,*
>   *vanilla, lemon juice, lime juice or*
>   *orange juice (NB: the flavour will*
>   *concentrate as it dries)*
> **icing sugar, for dusting**

Preheat your oven or dehydrator to 70°C and lay a piece of baking parchment (or resusable silicone paper) on your work surface. (Do not use wax paper or foil; wax paper will melt and foil will get too hot and cook the leather.)

Wash your fruit thoroughly, remove any stems, cores, seeds or stones and peel if necessary. Fruit like apples will need heating, raspberries can just be mashed raw. Cut the fruit into chunks and place in a heavy-based saucepan. Splash in a little water, cover with a lid and set over a low heat until the fruit collapses. Mash with a potato masher or blitz in a food-processor to a smooth purée. Stir in the lemon juice or citric acid (which will stop the fruit discolouring) and the sugar (or honey) and flavourings. The mixture should be syrupy, the consistency of runny honey, if it's too wet, cook it slightly to reduce the water content.

Spread the purée over the prepared baking parchment, roughly 0.5cm thick when poured (it will shrink). You can go thicker but it will take longer to dry. The leather dries from the outside edge in. It is dry when the middle is no longer sticky. Push the centre with your fingers; if you see an indent it needs longer to dry. How long it takes depends largely on the size, thickness and water content of the fruit, but expect 8 hours in a dehydrator at 70°C or 18 hours in your oven; consider the cost of that and a dehydrator becomes a worthwhile investment if you are going to make lots. You can use a solar dehydrator, but you need long, hot days for this to work.

Once your leathers are dry, cut or rip them into strips, then dust with icing sugar to stop them sticking together, if you like, and wrap in plastic or store in an airtight container (they need to be kept dry to store well). This way they will store for a month at room temperature, several months at 10°C and forever (or at least a year) in the freezer.

STRAWBERRY FRUIT LEATHER

There is more lemon juice in this recipe because the banana tends to brown without it and I personally like the tang. Add the lemon juice last as you see fit.

1kg ripe strawberries
440g granulated sugar (or to taste)
3–4 mint leaves or some freshly ground
    black pepper (optional)
juice of 1 small lemon
2 very ripe bananas (optional)
icing sugar, for dusting

Preheat a dehydrator to 70°C, or set your oven to its lowest setting. Wash the strawberries and cut into quarters. Place in a bowl, pour over the granulated sugar and set aside for 1–2 hours to draw out the juices.

Mash with a potato masher to purée the fruit; I like mine quite smooth. Alternatively, blitz in a food-processor along with a few mint leaves (if using). Squeeze over the lemon juice and season with black pepper (optional). If your mixture looks quite runny at this stage you can bulk it up with some mashed banana (which will also help to sweeten the leather).

Ladle the strawberry purée on to a sheet of baking parchment (or reusable silicone paper) to a thickness of 5–8mm and transfer to your dehydrator or oven. The length of time the leather will take to dry will depend on the temperature, but 7 hours should be sufficient in a dehydrator; an oven will take longer. Once the leather is dry to the touch, cut it into strips and dust with icing sugar. Store in an airtight container.

How to dry vegetables

BEANS: *see page 63*

BEETROOT: blanch or steam them whole in boiling water for 10–15 minutes, until just tender, then cut into 0.5cm slices. Dry until crisp, but still bend rather than snap (timing will depend on the freshness of the beet, but expect 7 hours or so). Store in an airtight container.

CHILLIES: spread out on a baking sheet or rack and dry at 70–80°C for 6–10 hours. Store in an airtight container in a cool place out of direct sunlight.
Note: if you are drying lots of chillies, say every tray stacked full, the heat of the oven or dehydrator will cause the chillies to release their oil. We woke one night quite sure that the end of the world had come as we choked on hot air, until I raced downstairs to shut off the machine!

GARLIC: slice or dice to the size you want for the recipe, as once dried, garlic is difficult to cut up. Spread out on a baking sheet or rack and dry at 60°C until the garlic is just dry and is still slightly pliable, watching carefully so that thinner pieces don't brown. Best used in salt and herb mixes.

TOMATOES: leave cherry tomatoes whole; halve larger tomatoes. Spread out on a baking sheet or rack, placing halved tomatoes cut-side up initially and turning halfway. Dry at 70–80°C. As each tomato is a little different in size, you will need to manage the situation by flipping and rearranging the trays to get an even finish; drying will take 4–12 hours. Dried tomatoes are a very good substitute for fresh, particularly for pasta sauces, stews and soups. They taste much like shop-bought sundried tomatoes, intensely sweet and chewy. Store in an airtight container in a cool place out of direct sunlight or in the freezer (where they will keep indefinitely).

VEGGIE CHIPS

Now I've always found plain old dried vegetables a little bit boring – that is,
until I stumbled across veggie chips. It all started with kale and now I can't stop.

KALE CHIPS

Making someone who hates greens eat highly nutritious kale is torture for all involved, and it doesn't matter how tiny you cut it up – that bitter flavour of the brassica family is just not for everyone (it turns out you either have a gene that makes you sensitive to this flavour of brassica or you don't, it is that simple). Kale chips proudly defy genes though; I haven't found a single person who doesn't like them (particularly if they are not told they are made out of kale).

You can try making these in your oven on the lowest setting, perhaps just with the pilot light, but you will have to check them regularly and turn them to stop them burning. A dehydrator is infinitely easier.

> **big bunch of kale, washed, dried, mid-ribs removed and torn into shreds about 4cm or so wide**
> **1 tablespoon cider vinegar**
> **½ teaspoon finely ground sea salt**
> **1 tablespoon olive or sunflower oil**
> **½ teaspoon chilli powder (optional)**
> **4 heaped tablespoons brewer's/ nutritional yeast (available from health food shops)** – *this is optional, but I think it makes them taste great*

Preheat your dehydrator to 70°C or turn your oven to the lowest setting. Place the kale in a large bowl and add the vinegar, salt, oil, chilli and brewer's yeast (if using). Mix everything really well to coat the kale all over and set aside to marinate for 1 hour.

Spread the chips out on the rack of your dehydrator (or on a baking tray if you are using the oven) and dry for 40 minutes.

FOR AN ASIAN TWIST try this marinade: 1 tablespoon cider vinegar, 1 tablespoon toasted sesame oil, ½ teaspoon soy sauce, 4 tablespoons brewer's yeast (optional).

COURGETTE OR BEETROOT CHIPS

You will need a mandolin to slice the chips thinly; aim for 5mm thick. If you don't own one of these, and you can't cut your slices thin enough by hand, blanch thicker slices in boiling water (or stock) for a minute or two before drying. You can make a salt and vinegar version by omitting the peppers and adding a teaspoon of cider vinegar. Carrot and parsnip chips can be treated similarly, but should be blanched in boiling water for 2 minutes before drying.

> 2 courgettes (or 2 large beetroots), washed and cut into slices with a mandolin
> 1 teaspoon olive or sunflower oil
> ¼ teaspoon finely ground sea salt
> ¼ teaspoon ground black pepper
> ¼ teaspoon smoked paprika *(or hot paprika if a kick is what you are looking for)*, optional

Preheat your dehydrator to 70°C or turn your oven to the lowest setting. Combine all the ingredients in a bowl and mix thoroughly with your hands to coat the chips all over. Set aside to marinate for at least an hour.

Spread the chips out on the rack of your dehydrator (or on a baking tray if you are using the oven) and dry for 4 hours until crisp.

Set aside to cool and store in an airtight container out of direct sunlight; they will keep for up to a month.

How to dry nuts

WALNUTS: remove the fleshy husks (or they will rot), spread out on a rack and allow to dry naturally (under cover if the weather is wet). Store in an airtight container in a cool, dry place for up to 2 years.

HAZELNUTS AND FILBERTS: spread out on a rack and allow to dry naturally (under cover if the weather is wet). Store in an airtight container. Once dried they will store for years.

SWEET CHESTNUTS: fresh (undried) chestnuts should be stored somewhere humid and cool; they will only store for a few weeks. To increase their storage life, deshell and dry in a dehydrator. Once completely dry, they will store for years. Dried sweet chestnuts are excellent ground and added to biscuits, pancakes and pasta; a coffee grinder should do the trick.

ON PICKLING

I love pickles and often crave their vinegary juices. My love for pickles is deep within my blood, inherited from my father who I know feels the same way about vinegar as I do. On any given morning, the smear of beetroot juice is found on my parents' kitchen table as my father's favourite midnight snack is pickled beetroot. He cannot get enough and it, in turn, cannot help but give him up as his hunger stains the table.

Fermenting may be a more noble preservation than pickling, but the speed and ease of a good pickle means that for those with little time, the immediate nature of warm vinegar, perhaps a little sugar, some salt and spices means that you can take your seasonal to year round in a matter of 30 minutes or so.

I think a good pickle should still speak of where it came from; it should be enlivened by the vinegar rather than overwhelmed by it. You shouldn't over pucker at the mere opening of a jar, it should be spicy and err on the pleasant side of acidic. Pickles should look bright and appealing, the brine shouldn't swim in too much cloudiness. Good pickles should invite an opening, they are there to revive tired dishes. I think pickled chillies (see page 83), particularly jalapeños, are wonderfully versatile. Try them not just on tacos, but also in cold pasta salads, sandwiches, with cheese or among sautéed greens. And once the pickle is used up, don't waste this good vinegar that can make all manner of vinaigrettes more interesting.

ON VINEGAR

Traditionally malt vinegar is required and there are times when its deep-brown chip shop flavour is lovely, but I think it's a mistake to stick only to this. Try rice wine vinegar for Asian pickles, white wine for pale vegetables, and red wine for deeper colours, or balsamic for tiny pearl onions. Or try cider vinegar sweetened with apple juice concentrate – a fine marriage indeed for a fruity brine – over thinly sliced courgette or cucumber with garlic and peppercorns for a perfect quick relish on roast chicken sandwiches.

You'll find some recipes call for packing the jar with boiling vinegar, particularly in older books. This method usually applies to long storage and tends to be for robust pickles, such as beetroot (which is cooked first).

While many people choose to waterbathe their finished jars of pickle (see page 157) to pasteurise the contents, this shouldn't be necessary if your vegetables are pickled in a suitably acidic solution. Traditionally in America, pickles are waterbathed to pasteurise the solution. I think to most European preservers this is a little baffling, but if you are the sort to not trust the strength of vinegar then pasteurisation is perhaps the best belt-and-braces solution. A low temperature pasteurisation in a waterbath (see bottling section) between 82°C/180°F and 85°C/185°F for 30 minutes is ideal. This is certainly true if you want to keep your pickles for more than a month or so.

To guarantee acidity, never reduce the amount/proportion of vinegar called for in a recipe. As a rule of thumb, you should always use at least as much vinegar as water, and you should always choose a vinegar with at least 5 and 6 per cent acidity. Don't skimp on the quality of the vinegar; it needs to be high grade. (And be wary of using homemade vinegar unless you can accurately check the acidity, the pH level could be weak and this will allow for pathogens to grow in your pickle). If your recipe is too tart, amend the recipe by adding more sugar; never water down the vinegar (the basic ratio is 60g sugar to 1 litre vinegar). If you choose to flout this rule, you will need to store the pickle in a fridge and should consume it within a week – or alternatively, pasteurise it by waterbathing.

Making herb vinegar

Herb vinegars make for great vinaigrettes, which in turn make for greater salads. The rule is to allow the flowers or petals to marinate for no longer than 2–3 weeks; leaves are tougher and can stay in for longer, but they will lose their colour and may disintegrate, which will affect the quality of the vinegar. I tend to use good-quality white wine or cider vinegar, as you don't want the vinegar to have an overpowering flavour to start with.

You can make herb vinegars from whatever pleases you, experimenting is half the fun, but here are some suggested flavourings: chive flowers (as above), garlic flowers, rose petals (always use white wine vinegar), dill seeds or leaves, fennel seeds and leaves, tarragon, fresh raspberries or redcurrants.

Note: Always wash flowers, petals and leaves first and allow them to dry naturally or the excess water will dilute the vinegar and shorten its shelf life.

On flavour

While many people adhere to the old adage that pickles should sit to improve their flavour, I find I enjoy them most when they are fresh, within a few hours of pickling, when I can really admire their crunch, or after a month or so at most when their flavours have emboldened slightly but they are still crisp. Commercial pickles contain additives to keep their crunch, but this isn't generally the case with homemade pickles, which can quickly lose their crispness and often turn to mush if left to sit for months. I think one solution is to eat them up quickly, keeping them for no more than three months – that way, they will easily see you through winter so you can move on to new flavours in spring. The Japanese understand this, pickling for one night, one week and perhaps one month – but never to sit on a shelf for more than a year.

How pickling works

Unlike fermenting, where the brine lowers the pH over a long period of time until the vegetables are preserved, with pickling this occurs instantly. The vinegar is so acidic it halts the spoilage microbes immediately to stop them getting a foothold.

ON BRINING

Brining your vegetables before pickling really does improve their texture, since it draws out excess water. I use two methods: brining in saltwater and dry-salting.

Brining works well for beetroot, cauliflower and fruit. I tend to brine overnight, though some recipes call for a two-day brine. To make a basic cold water brine, you will need a ratio of 100g salt to 1 litre water. Simply heat the salt in the water, stirring until it dissolves, and set aside to cool before immersing the vegetables.

Dry-salting works best for vegetables with a high percentage of water, such as cucumbers, courgettes and marrows (I use this method for smaller batches of pickle). All you need to do is sprinkle some salt over your vegetables and weigh them down with a plate (perhaps with a few weights on top to speed things up). I find it draws out just as much liquid as brining, and because you rinse off the salt afterwards you don't have to be too fussy about measuring. For large quantities of vegetables, you should layer them up with salt in between the layers.

ON SPICES

All manner of spices can be added to flavour the vinegar. For best results, make up the vinegar solution a week or so before pickling to give the spices time to mingle together and gently flavour the vinegar. If you forget to do this, you can take a shortcut by very gently and slowly heating the vinegar with the spices to draw out the flavours. For sweet vinegar, add the sugar two weeks prior to pickling, gently shaking the bottle every day until the sugar is dissolved.

Whole spices are considered superior to ground because ground spices tend to cloud the vinegar; if a recipe calls for whole and you only have ground, use a quarter of the amount called for. Many recipes suggest you strain out the spices before bottling.

This is entirely up to you, but clearly if you leave the spices in they will continue to infuse the vinegar – something to consider if you are opening that long-forgotten jar; it might kick back a bit. If you are using ground spices, you will need to strain through layers of muslin.

MAKING YOUR OWN SPICE MIXES One of the joys of pickling is adapting and experimenting with your own spice mixes. Toasting the spices beforehand in a hot pan enhances their flavour, adding a lovely rich note to the vinegar. I particularly like cumin, coriander, mustard and fennel seed in equal parts, toasted on a hot skillet until the seeds release their aromas and just start to colour.

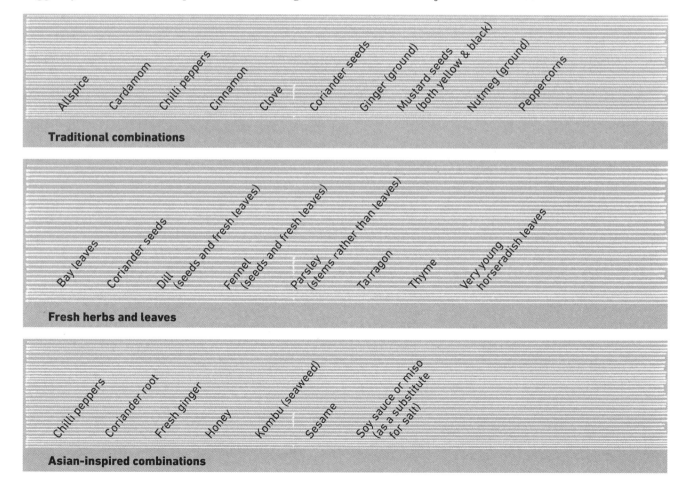

Traditional combinations

Allspice · Cardamom · Chilli peppers · Cinnamon · Clove · Coriander seeds · Ginger (ground) · Mustard seeds (both yellow & black) · Nutmeg (ground) · Peppercorns

Fresh herbs and leaves

Bay leaves · Coriander seeds · Dill (seeds and fresh leaves) · Fennel (seeds and fresh leaves) · Parsley (stems rather than leaves) · Tarragon · Thyme · Very young horseradish leaves

Asian-inspired combinations

Chilli peppers · Coriander root · Fresh ginger · Honey · Kombu (seaweed) · Sesame · Soy sauce or miso (as a substitute for salt)

PICKLED FENNEL

This was inspired by an anniversary dinner at a local restaurant. We ate succulent duck served with pickled fennel and grapefruit segments. I loved how the crunchy fennel and grapefruit were used to lift the meat. With no grapefruit to hand, I substituted orange and added a few spices to up the game.

As with all pickles, the vinegar and salt ratio is essential for preservation – but the rest is up to you. Omit the coriander, add a little lemon juice or use pink peppercorns instead of black. It's your pickle, not mine, so be inventive.

200ml white wine vinegar
4 tablespoons orange juice
4 tablespoons granulated sugar
1½ teaspoons salt
pinch of peppercorns
pinch of coriander seeds
pinch of fennel seeds
2 small fennel bulbs, finely sliced, plus a
   few fronds for good measure
sterilised jars with lids (see page 138);
   how many depends on the size of your
   jars

Place the vinegar, fruit juice, sugar, salt and spices in a large pan and briefly bring to boil. Meanwhile, pack the sliced fennel into your sterilised jars. Pour the hot pickling liquor over the packed fennel and put on the lids immediately; set aside to cool. I don't bother to strain the pickling solution as I like the flavours to intensify.

Store in a cool place out of direct sunlight. Once opened, you should store the pickle in the fridge and eat it up within 2 weeks.

Note: this pickle is not the sort to hide at the back of the cupboard, as the fennel will lose its crunch after a few weeks, so eat it up sooner rather than later. To keep the crunch a bit longer, try brining the fennel overnight (see page 77) or pop a grape leaf in the jar (see right).

Keeping the crunch

A traditional method of keeping pickles crunchy is to include a young, fresh grape leaf in the pickling jar. Grape leaves are naturally rich in tannin, which helps to keep the contents crisp, and they are also thought to keep the colour bright. I have also read that currant, white oak and cherry leaves can be used, but I imagine they might impart a flavour to the pickle. Just make sure you wash the leaf beforehand. Small leaves can be tucked in first at the bottom of the jar; I find larger leaves are better placed on the surface as they stop the vegetables from floating to the top.

PICKLED MUSTARD GREENS JAPANESE STYLE

In Japan this is traditionally eaten with rice as an after-school snack. I find it rocks with fried rice, although I sometimes feel it would benefit from being a bit sweeter.

200g greens (mustard, radish tops or
  Oriental greens)
45ml dark soy sauce
45ml white wine or rice vinegar
10–20g sugar *(I use 20g brown sugar)*
1–2 small hot fresh chillies, *left whole for
  a mild kick or chopped for some heat,
  as you see fit*
1 x 5cm piece of fresh ginger, finely
  grated or minced
sterilised jars with lids (see page 138);
  *how many depends on the size of your
  jars*

Wash your greens and dry them thoroughly overnight (this is important because any excess water will dilute the vinegar).

Cut your greens into bite-sized pieces and pack them into your sterilised jars. Combine the soy sauce, vinegar, sugar, chillies and ginger in a large jug and stir until the sugar dissolves; if it won't dissolve, heat everything gently together in a medium pan and set aside to cool.

Pour the liquid over the greens so that they are fully covered and put on the lids. You will have to weigh down the greens so that they are covered. This can be done with a very clean stone, washed and then boiled for 30 minutes. After 48 hours, you should be able to remove the stones as the greens should be now fully submerged (ie. they've absorbed the soy sauce and should sink). Store in the fridge.

PICKLED WILD GARLIC KOREAN STYLE

Now I have to admit that this is an interpretation, as I couldn't find any exact recipes (or quite understand the translations) so I made it up as best I could. Still, the results are sublime – sweet, salty garlic heaven.

Use equal parts of rice vinegar, sugar, soy sauce and water heated together and allowed to cool slightly. You need a large bunch of wild garlic roots trimmed off and well washed. Allow the garlic to dry first as any excess water will affect the recipe.

Once the pickle mixture has cooled, but is still warm, pour three-quarters of the mixture over the wild garlic and allow to sit for three days or so. I use a crock with weights to keep the garlic from floating. Keep the reserved liquid in the fridge. After three days the garlic should have wilted and can be packed tightly into a glass jar and topped up with the remaining liquid and stored in the fridge in an airtight container.

These pickles are great with rice, in stir-fries, chopped up in salad or used in tempura. It's become a must-have in a smoked tofu sandwich; in fact I'd stick it on top of ice-cream if I could get away with it.

PICKLED JERUSALEM ARTICHOKES

I soak the sliced chokes in brine for 18 hours (you can leave them for up to 24 hours if necessary) first. This keeps the chokes incredibly crispy and allows them to store for longer. If you don't have time to do this, then they will have to be stored in the fridge, as the water content of the chokes will affect pickling. Not that this matters much as they make a lovely quick pickle. Substitute this pickle for any gherkin/cucumber pickle you might use, say in a roasted chicken sandwich, with pâtés or goulash.

700g Jerusalem artichokes, peeled and
thinly sliced (no more than 5mm thick)
300ml cider (or white wine) vinegar
50ml water
1 tablespoon whole coriander seeds
1 teaspoon whole peppercorns
¼ teaspoon ground turmeric
1 teaspoon cumin seeds
¼ teaspoon ground ginger (or 4–5 thin
slices fresh root ginger)
2 heaped tablespoons brown sugar
2 bay leaves
sterilised jars with lids (see page 138);
*how many depends on the size of
your jars*

Soak your sliced artichokes in brine for 24 hours (see page 77); taste and if too salty give them a quick rinse. Dry thoroughly.

Place the remaining ingredients in a large pan and bring to the boil, stirring to dissolve the sugar.

Pack the artichokes into sterilised jars and pour over the pickling solution so they are fully covered. Store in a cool, dark place for at least a week before eating.

PICKLED CHILLIES

You can use any chillies for this recipe, but I find the thick-skinned varieties such as habañeros, rocotos or padrons tend to work best. I warn against the use of super-hot varieties such as bird's eye or Dorset naga, since the vinegar seems to turn them molten. If you really want to use them, because molten is the only way you taste food, don't finely chop them up first, just slice into even rounds.

Don't waste the vinegar solution once you've eaten all the chillies; it makes a great marinade for roasted vegetables or barbecued meat.

whole chillies
white wine vinegar
water
sea salt (not table)
sugar
sterilised jar and lid (see page 138)

As everyone's chillies are different sizes, particularly if you are growing more than one variety, then the simplest way to make this recipe is to measure the volume of liquid it takes to fill your jar, once packed with chillies (consider this rinsing the chillies if you like). Pour out this water and measure it. You need equal parts water and vinegar so pour half away and the rest into a pan to heat.

For every 250ml of liquid, you need 2 teaspoons salt (not table salt) and 2 teaspoons sugar (though you can use less if you wish).

To this basic vinegar solution, you can add all manner of spices. I think a clove of garlic and a bay leaf per jar is a must. Otherwise, consider adding coriander and cumin seed, perhaps some fresh marjoram and peppercorns. Heat the solution and pour over the chillies, cover and seal. The flavour of the chillies improves greatly with time, so wait a week before eating. If you want to store them for a long time I suggest waterbathing at 82–85°C for 30 minutes.

COURGETTE PICKLE

This pickle should be stored in the fridge and used within a month. You can substitute sliced cucumbers if you wish.

6 courgettes
a small handful of raisins
sea salt, for brining
250ml cider vinegar
250ml apple juice
3 teaspoons sea salt
approx. 200g sugar (or 125ml
    concentrated apple juice), to taste
1 bay leaf, crushed
1 sweet onion, finely sliced
pinch of black peppercorns
3 garlic cloves, thinly sliced (optional)
sprig of dill, torn into pieces
500ml sterilised jar with lid (see page
    138)

Wash the courgettes, dry thoroughly and cut into very thin rounds using a mandolin or potato peeler. The aim is to have translucent slices.

Place the courgettes in a bowl, add the raisins and cover with a layer of salt. Cover the courgettes with a plate and weigh down with another bowl filled with water if necessary. Set aside to marinate for at least 30 minutes, preferably overnight.

The following morning, tip the courgettes into a colander and rinse off the salt. Dry the courgettes thoroughly and pack them into a sterilised jar.

Place the vinegar, apple juice, salt, sugar (or apple concentrate), bay leaf, sliced onion, peppercorns, garlic (if using) and dill in a large saucepan. Bring to the boil, stirring to dissolve the sugar, and then set aside to cool slightly (this is important or the boiling liquor will turn the courgettes to mush).

Pour the warm liquor over the courgettes in the jar, making sure that it covers them completely. I sometimes pop a grape leaf on top to stop the ingredients from floating to the surface (see page 79).

PICKLED CHERRY TOMATOES OR TOMATILLOS

You can use a mixture of tomatoes and tomatillos for this recipe, just make sure they are all roughly the same size. Green or red tomatoes both work well, but avoid using overripe fruit. I like a single cherry tomato in a Bloody Mary.

450g small cherry tomatoes
4 tarragon leaves
4 black peppercorns
4 coriander seeds
a good pinch of sea salt, to taste
white wine vinegar
sugar, to taste *(optional, but usually
    needed for green tomatoes)*
a needle
500ml sterilised jar with lid (see page
    138)

Gently wash the tomatoes, taking care not to burst them. Prick each one 2–3 times with a needle to encourage them to absorb the pickling solution. Pack into a sterilised jar.

Wash the tarragon leaves and dry them carefully on kitchen paper. Pop them into the jar with the tomatoes and put in the peppercorns, coriander seeds, a good pinch of salt and some sugar, if using. Pour over enough vinegar to cover and screw on the lids. Store in a cool, dark place for up to six months.

BEER-BRINED PICKLES

The next two recipes are inspired by the microbreweries of Seattle where any excuse for pairing something with beer is par for the course. These pickles are subtle, there's no strong vinegar kick (and for that reason they won't store for ever).

You could pickle any number of vegetables in this way, but I find cauliflower, French beans, carrots, green tomatoes, cucumbers, beetroot and tomatillos work best. Enjoy these pickles in sandwiches, with cheese and crackers and, of course, as an accompaniment to drinking beer.

BEER-BRINED CAULI PICKLE (VERSION 1)

I've used a malty British beer here along with malt vinegar, but you could use any deep-bodied beer (nothing bitter tasting) and substitute the malt vinegar for white wine vinegar for a less heavy smoky flavour. I've gone for an overnight brine because it means you don't have to boil up your vegetables to get them to soften; it also means they absorb more pickle while still having crunch. This recipe also works with French beans. When packing these into the jar, it's easiest to lay it on its side and slide the beans in like sardines.

> 1 head of cauliflower
> 400ml malty beer – *I used 'Old Dan'*
> 400ml water
> 400ml malt vinegar
> 2 tablespoons brown sugar
> 1 teaspoon mustard seeds
> 1 bay leaf
> 1 teaspoon black peppercorns
> 3 garlic cloves, peeled and scored with a
>   cross at one end *(this draws the pickling
>   juices inside, making for a sweeter bite)*
> 1 hot green chilli, sliced
> 1½ teaspoons sea salt
> sterilised jar with a lid (see page 138)

Break the cauliflower into florets and soak overnight in a brining solution (see page 77); taste a little bit and if they are too salty, rinse and drain.

The following morning, place the beer and water in a large pan and bring to the boil; boil rapidly for 5 minutes to burn off some of the alcohol. If you want your cauliflower florets to soften slightly, add them to the pan and cook briefly for 2–3 minutes (you don't want them to turn to mush); remove with a slotted spoon.

Add the vinegar, sugar, salt and flavourings to the pan, stirring to dissolve the sugar. Bring to the boil and boil rapidly for 5 minutes. Taste and adjust the seasoning if you wish.

Pack the cauliflower florets into a sterilised jar. Pour in the hot pickling liquor so that it covers the vegetables completely by at least 1cm. Put on the lid and set aside to cool. For best results, wait for at least 24 hours before eating to allow the flavours to develop. Store in the fridge for up to 6 weeks.

BEER-BRINED CAULI PICKLE (VERSION 2)

This recipe hangs on the flavour of fresh coriander. Coriander root is very hard to buy, but if you grow your own you should have access to both the seed and the root by the end of summer. If you have trouble obtaining it, simply add some toasted coriander seeds in with the fennel seeds instead.

> 1 head of cauliflower
> sea salt for brining
> 400ml medium-bodied beer
>   – *I used Adnams*
> 400ml water
> 400ml white wine vinegar
> 1 teaspoon honey (optional)
> 3 x 5cm pieces of coriander root
> 2 teaspoons fresh green coriander seeds
> 4 teaspoons mustard seeds

4 teaspoons fennel seeds

4 small red/green chillies

2 teaspoons fresh thyme leaves

3–4 garlic cloves, peeled and scored with
a cross at one end *(this draws the
pickle's juices inside, making for a
sweeter bite)*

1 bay leaf

sterilised jar with lid (see page 138)

Break the cauliflower into florets and soak
overnight in a brining solution (see page 77). (If you
don't have time for this, add a further 3 tablespoons
salt to the vinegar solution.)

The following morning, place the beer and water
in a large pan and bring to the boil; boil rapidly for
5 minutes to burn off some of the alcohol. Add the
cauliflower florets and cook briefly for 2–3 minutes
to soften them slightly; remove with a slotted spoon.
Add the vinegar, honey, coriander root and salt to

the pan and boil rapidly for 5 minutes. Taste and
adjust the seasoning if necessary.

In a large, heavy-based pan, toast the coriander,
mustard and fennel seeds over a high heat until you
hear the mustard pop. Quickly pour in the hot
pickling solution and bring back to the boil. Simmer
gently for 10 minutes to release the flavours. Taste
and adjust the seasoning if necessary, adding a bit
more honey or sugar if the liquid tastes too tart.

Pack the cauliflower florets into your sterilised
jar and pour over the hot pickling liquor so that it
covers them completely. Add the chillies, thyme,
garlic and bay leaf. (I also like to insert a grape leaf
to prevent the cauliflower florets from floating to
the surface (see page 79); this also keeps the pickle
crisp. Put on the lids and set aside to cool. Store in
the refrigerator for at least 24 hours to allow the
flavours to develop before eating.

Relishes and chutney are very similar and the term is used interchangeably. Relishes tend to be more finely textured. Unlike jam, there is no setting point with a chutney or relish; once the ingredients are cooked down harmoniously they are simply potted up in clean jars and stored.

Many chutney recipes are bulked out with tomatoes, marrow or apples to make them go further, especially if there isn't enough natural juice in the other vegetables they are cooked with. The drawback of bulking them out with apples is that your chutney normally ends up a rather sludgy brown colour, so if you want your chutney to remain green leave out the apples.

Just like pickling recipes, most good chutney recipes are not written in stone; you can adapt them to suit your ingredients. I've used dried blueberries where a recipe has called for currants, changed cider vinegar for wine, added more chillies and less cloves, all successfully. This is your opportunity to get rid of gluts of tomatoes or marrows and use up odds and ends; just make sure you add enough vinegar and sugar to make it something special.

How to make chutney

As a general rule of thumb, for every 1kg of fruit/ vegetables you will need 5g salt, 100g sugar and 125–250ml vinegar. Cut everything up the same size so it cooks evenly and then simmer with the rest of the ingredients until your vegetables are tender but still hold their shape. It's as simple as that!

There's nothing complicated about making chutneys, but the process cannot be rushed. A mellow flavoured chutney requires long, gentle cooking, around 2 hours, plus time for the flavour to develop in the jar (4 weeks at least). A simple green tomato chutney might take around 30 minutes, but for Jerusalem artichokes you're looking at somewhere nearer to 3 hours – that's a lot of stirring, so invite some friends over.

Never use copper pans as they give an un-pleasant metallic taste to the chutney. Vinegar has a hardening effect, particularly on onions and garlic, so don't add these raw just before bottling. (If you decide that you need more onion, garlic or even apples, always soften them down fully first in another pan before stirring them into your chutney.)

On sugar

If you want dark chutney, use brown sugar; if you want light chutney, use white or light brown. The longer you cook the sugar, the darker your chutney will become. If you want a particularly light coloured version, you should cook all the basic ingredients first until soft before adding the sugar.

BEETROOT MARMALADE

This sweet, caramelised relish sits perfectly with grilled goat's cheese or a ploughman's. By roasting the beetroot first, you enhance its earthy flavours. I tend to roast it the night before, adding a few extra beetroots to the pan to serve as a light supper alongside couscous and perhaps a little feta as a warm salad. Then the next morning you can whiz through the next stage.

1kg beetroot
100ml balsamic vinegar
a handful each of fresh marjoram and
     thyme leaves
sea salt, to taste
zest and juice of 1 large orange
2 large red onions, finely diced
50g light brown sugar
2 tablespoons olive oil
4 garlic cloves, peeled and sliced
100g caster sugar
400ml red wine vinegar
sterilised jars with lids (see page 138);
     how many depends on the size of
     your jars

Preheat the oven to 160°C. Wash and peel the beetroot and cut into quarters. Place in a roasting tin with the balsamic vinegar, marjoram and thyme leaves, add a pinch of sea salt and grate over the orange zest (set aside the juice for later). Mix everything together with your hands to coat the beetroots all over, cover with foil and roast for 40 minutes or until you can pierce the beetroot with a knife; set aside to cool completely.

The following morning, coarsely grate the beetroot into a bowl, scraping in any juices from the roasting tin; set aside.

Place the diced red onions in a large, heavy-based pan with the light brown sugar and olive oil. Set over a very low heat and stir gently until the onions soften completely and start to caramelise. Add the sliced garlic, grated beetroot, caster sugar, orange juice and red wine vinegar. Cook on a gentle simmer for 30 minutes until the liquid has reduced by about two-thirds, stirring from time to time to stop it from sticking. You can tell when the relish is cooked because you will be able to draw a spoon across the bottom of the pan and it will initially stay clear before refilling with syrupy juices. If there are no juices, it means you've overcooked your relish; add a little more vinegar (or orange juice if you have some) and perhaps a touch of sugar and cook briefly to rehydrate the mixture.

Scoop the hot relish into sterilised jars while it is still hot, cover with wax discs and put on the lids. Store in a cool, dark place for up to 6 months.

JERUSALEM ARTICHOKE CHUTNEY

If you grow Jerusalem artichokes, by their nature you will usually end up with too many. When you're bored to death of soufflés, soups or chips, try this chutney. It's really something you'll look forward to eating. It is quite spicy with a bit of a kick back, due to the mustard, because I like it that way. If you prefer something milder, halve the amount of chilli and mustard seeds. I have, in the past, omitted the apples and used chopped cabbage instead, which worked well. It is good under a baked egg in a ramekin with a little grated cheese on top.

  1.1kg Jerusalem artichokes, peeled and
    cut into 1cm chunks
  225g apples, peeled and cut into 1cm
    chunks
  6 garlic cloves, sliced
  1 onion, sliced or diced
  5 small red chillies, finely sliced
  25g sea salt
  4 heaped tablespoons mustard seeds
  1 tablespoon turmeric powder
  1 tablespoon mixed pickling spices
    *(coriander, allspice, peppercorns,
    cloves, ginger, mustard seeds)*
  1 tablespoon celery seeds
  water (or cider), to cover
  600ml cider vinegar
  400–450g soft brown sugar
  sterilised jars with lids (see page 138);
    *how many depends on the size of
    your jars*

If you wish, you can soak the Jerusalem artichokes in brine overnight (see page 77); this will help to preserve their crispness.

Drain the Jerusalem artichokes and place in a large pan with the apples, garlic, onion, chillies, salt and spices. Cover with water (or cider) and cook over a low heat until the apples and onions are soft, but the chokes are still crisp. For me, the joy of this chutney is that the chokes still have a bite at the end. (If you think this is a strange idea, you could keep cooking everything to a mush.)

Add the vinegar and sugar and stir to dissolve the sugar. Bring to the boil, stirring all the time, and simmer until the mixture thickens; this could take up to 3 hours. Once the chutney is ready, you should be able to draw a wooden spoon across the base of the pan so that it clears, but quickly refills with syrupy juices.

Bottle up in sterilised jars (see page 138) and cover with wax discs and lids. Store in a cool dark place. Wait at least 4 weeks before eating so that it can mellow.

GREEN TOMATO CHUTNEY

I prefer to make this chutney with cherry tomatoes, cooking them down slowly and gently so that the toms remain almost whole. If you want a very green tomato chutney, omit the apples and up the amount of green tomatoes.

  450g apples, peeled, cored and chopped
    *(save the cores and peels for making
    pectin, see page 130)*
  3 large onions (preferably red) or 450g
    shallots, diced
  1.3kg green tomatoes *(kept whole if using
    cherries, otherwise halved or chopped)*
  200g raisins *(or a mixture of dried
    cranberries/blueberries and
    elderberries – essentially whatever
    sweet dried fruit you have to hand)*
  15g finely chopped root ginger
  8–10 small red chillies *(deseeded if you
    don't want it too hot)*, chopped
  6 garlic cloves, peeled and sliced
  2 teaspoons black peppercorns
  600ml white wine vinegar
  450g light brown sugar
  2 teaspoons sea salt
  sterilised jars with lids (page 138); *how
    many depends on the size of your jars*

Place the apples in a large, heavy-based pan with a scant amount of water (to stop them catching) and heat until they start to soften. Put in the onions, tomatoes, raisins, ginger, chillies, garlic and peppercorns and cook over a low heat until the tomatoes start to collapse and soften, about 15 minutes.

Pour in the vinegar and add the sugar and salt, stirring to dissolve. Bring to the boil stirring constantly and simmer until you have a thick consistency. You should by the end be able to draw a spoon across the bottom of the pan so that it clears, but rapidly refills with syrupy juices. Ladle into hot, sterilised jars, cover with wax discs and lids, label and store. This chutney will keep for 6 months in a cool, dark place.

500g brown sugar

600ml cider vinegar

3–4 garlic cloves, sliced

2 teaspoons sea salt

2 teaspoons ground ginger

2 teaspoons mustard seeds

pinch of cayenne pepper

FOR THE SPICE BAG

3 teaspoons cloves (around 9 cloves)

1 teaspoon coriander seeds

1 teaspoon black peppercorns

1 cinnamon stick

sterilised jars with lids (see page 138);
how many depends on the size of your jars

Peel and dice the marrow, courgette or pumpkin, discarding the woody part and any large seeds. Place in a bowl and scatter over a couple of handfuls of salt, just enough so that all surfaces are lightly dusted. Set aside for at least 4 hours (preferably overnight) to draw out all the moisture. Rinse and pat dry. This dry-salting process keeps the marrow in good shape and stops it collapsing, otherwise it just turns to mush.

Make up your spice bag by putting the spices in a piece of muslin and tying them tightly with string.

Place all the remaining chutney ingredients in a heavy-based pan and bring to the boil, stirring to dissolve the sugar. Simmer gently, stirring from time to time, until the mixture is thick but not stiff, roughly 40 minutes or so. By the end you should be able to draw a spoon across the bottom of the pan so that it clears, but rapidly refills with syrupy juices.

Ladle the hot chutney into warm sterilised jars, cover with wax discs and put on the lids. Store somewhere cool and dark for at least 2 weeks before using. This chutney will keep well for up to 6 months.

PLOUGHMAN'S CHUTNEY

This one is for those 'gifted' marrows offered up as a bag of courgettes. It is particularly good slathered over turkey on Boxing Day or with strong English Cheddar.

1kg marrow, courgette or pumpkin

a couple of handfuls of salt

500g apples (or green tomatoes) cored, peeled and chopped

500g onions, roughly chopped

250g raisins, sultanas, currants or dried elderberries

What to do with all those tired jars of chutney?

We've all fallen into the trap of producing one too many jars of chutney – and when your guests preempt your offer to go home with some then you know you're in trouble. Learn from your mistakes and try to ring in the changes with small, varied batches rather than producing loads of bottles of the same thing. If all else fails and your jars of chutney start mounting up in the back of the larder, try the following:

I heard about this recipe on BBC 'Woman's Hour' and it works a treat. If you are bored to death of marrow chutney, or you've been gifted one too many jars, dump the entire jar into a stew or tagine; the spices and sweetness make for an extraordinary base. Add plenty of water to counterbalance the acidity and cook on a low heat for a long time.

Another favourite is Nigel Slater's recipe for baked egg and chutney. Spoon a dollop of good spicy chutney into the base of a ramekin, crack an egg on top and finish with a grating of cheese – Mr Slater calls for something fancy like Tallegio, but I've used everything from old Stilton to Cheddar. Pop in the oven at 180°C and bake until the top is bubbling and brown. Eat with good crusty bread.

What went wrong?

As with all home-preserving, successful pickling is all about trial and error. If things don't work out first time round, here are some suggestions for batch two:

Hard pickle: try pricking your fruit first before pickling (this encourages it to soak up the pickling liquor evenly).

Cloudy/ yeasty liquid: this is usually due to insufficient brining, use of hard water, or the spices not being strained from the liquid.

Vinegar separating from the chutney: this is usually because you didn't cook the chutney for long enough so it is hasn't thickened properly.

Shrinkage/drying out in the jar: usually a sign of a poor seal, or because you have left your chutney for way too long before eating. Your chutney needs to be liberated from the back of the cupboard!

On metallic lids

If you are reusing jars with metallic lids and they don't have non-reactive covers (the white bits), you should protect your chutney by covering it with a wax disc – otherwise the vinegar could corrode the metal. (This happens particularly with chutneys that are stored for long periods of time.) It is not wise to use metallic lids for pickles as the acid in the vinegar will most definitely corrode the lid, wax disc or not.

When to throw your chutney/pickle away

If you notice any of the following, it's time to dump your pickle on the compost pile:

» Gassiness (small bubbles)

» Mushy, slippery or just plain unappealing pickles

» Off-coloured pickles

» Any kind of unpleasant smell

» Mould (god knows how you got that to grow in vinegar, but you surely don't want to eat it)

For me that sour, salty taste of something fermented is a flavour I crave deeply. I can often be found eating kraut straight out of the jar at the fridge. I love the process of making pickles this way. It is both simple, requiring in its most basic form nothing more than wild yeasts in the air, yet its benefits are complex and deeply compelling at the same time. Fermented foods contain that rare and strange fifth flavour, umami, which is so addictive, but there is more to them than just a sensation – fermented foods are hugely important to our health, containing a unique mixture of good bacteria and vitamins.

Fermentation is one of the earliest methods of preserving food. In its simplest form, it requires nothing more than a pit in the ground and sometimes salt – no fuel and no cooking – and the advantage is it can be carried out in any climate (pit fermentation is predominately found down in the South Pacific and Ethiopia). It remains one of the most environmentally friendly ways to preserve your bounty. Fermented food can store for several months in cool conditions.

The process can be rapid, as in the Japanese Tsukemono method that ferments in a day, or take up to a month for slower ferments such as krauts.

How fermentation works

Fermentation works by encouraging certain good bacteria, such as *Lactobacillus plantarum,* to flourish and thus exclude bad bacteria and spoilage microbes. The good bacteria need anaerobic conditions in order to thrive. Under these conditions, the good bacteria get to invade the plant material first, outcompeting the bad bacteria (or creating an environment under which the bad bacteria cannot survive). Once inside the plant material, the good bacteria produce a variety of antimicrobial substances, mainly lactic acid, carbon dioxide and alcohol (bring on the beer!). The important part for the eater is that the vegetable and fruit are left intact with plenty of vitamin C. Sauerkraut has more vitamin C than fresh cabbage because the vitamin is protected from oxidation from the carbon dioxide produced by the good bacteria. Many fermented foods also contain significant amounts of B vitamins, which among other things give you healthy skin and hair, and are thought to protect you from pancreatic cancer.

These good bacteria are believed to have evolved from anaerobic piles of rotting vegetables. I love the fact that two of my favourite things in life, compost and pickles, come from the same place.

Although it is entirely possible to ferment using merely the plant's own juice – for example, when making Gundruk or sinki (a fermented radish root pickle) (see page 109) – most fermentation uses salt, along with chillies, herbs and sugars, to draw out the plant's natural juices and limit exposure to oxygen.

At low temperatures and salt levels, pickles are fermented by the unpronounceable microbes, *Leuconstoc mesenteroides;* at higher temperatures *Lactobacillus plantarum* are favoured. In ferments such as sauerkraut, *Leuconstoc mesenteroides* start the process because they can survive in more salty and sugary conditions. Once they get to work, they release carbon dioxide and other acids that lower the pH and turn the conditions anaerobic allowing *Lactobacillus plantarum* to move in and finish off the process. *Leuconstoc* smell bad and some are harmful to humans, therefore if your pickle starts smelling off it is probably because you have too much *Leuconstoc* and not enough *Lactobacillus.*

Whey is added to some pickles to increase the levels of lactic acid, which speeds up the process no end, but this does give a slightly different flavour.

Brine solutions

I know that a litre looks like a lot of brine solution, but most people don't have scales that can measure less than 5g of salt (unless you're a drug dealer), so for ease it needs to be a litre, and even I can figure out the maths required for a half or a quarter the amount.

BRINE SOLUTION: 10–20G SALT IN 1 LITRE OF WATER

1-2%
OF SALT

SUITABLE FOR:
CABBAGE OR TURNIP

MICROBES:
Lactic acid & Bacteria

TRADITIONAL NAME:
Sauerkraut

BRINE SOLUTION: 30–40G SALT IN 1 LITRE OF WATER

3-4%
OF SALT

SUITABLE FOR:
CABBAGE, RADISH, TURNIP, CHILLIES

MICROBES:
Lactic acid & Bacteria

TRADITIONAL NAME:
Kimchi

BRINE SOLUTION: 50–80G SALT IN 1 LITRE OF WATER

5-8%
OF SALT

SUITABLE FOR:
CUCUMBER

MICROBES:
Lactic acid & Bacteria

TRADITIONAL NAME:
Pickle

BRINE SOLUTION: 50–100G SALT IN 1 LITRE OF WATER

5-10%
OF SALT

SUITABLE FOR:
LEMONS OR LIMES

MICROBES:
Yeast

TRADITIONAL NAME:
Preserves lemons/limes

PRESERVED IN OWN JUICES; REQUIRES HEAT

0%
ENCLOSED JAR

SUITABLE FOR:
LEAFY VEGETABLES E.G. MUSTARD GREENS, SWISS CHARD ETC.

MICROBES:
Lactic acid

TRADITIONAL NAME:
Gundruk

Adapted from Harold McGee
On Food and Cooking
and G. Campbell-Platt
Fermented Foods of the World: A Dictionary and Guide

Troubleshooting the fermentation process

The most common issue with fermentation is vegetables floating to the top of the brine solution because they are not suitably weighed down, or the top layer becoming exposed to air due to lack of brine. Sometimes it is just a simple case of pressing down on the vegetables to coax out the brine, but at other times, when there is not enough brine, it might be necessary to top it up with a fresh solution of brine. Recipes vary and the brine solutions on page 97 should be used as a guide rather than a dictum, but if you do need to top up your brine solution stick to these percentages. Bear in mind that if your kraut dries out, the top layer will become exposed to air and undesirable microbes. Thin films of yeast, mould or bacteria, all of which require air to grow, can then enter the solution. The result is that the brine's acidity is lowered and spoilage microbes start to grow. This creates smelly, discoloured or soft pickles. If this occurs on day one or two – if your cabbage was simply not packed down with sufficient liquid, for example – you can correct this by adding brine. However, if it happens from day five onwards, spoilage will start to occur (particularly if you are fermenting in a warm room) and then you should compost your pickle because it will no longer be safe to eat.

How to stop your ferments from floating

Most vegetables need to be weighed down so that they remain fully submerged in the brine. Traditional sauerkraut pots come with two half moon ceramic weights, which need to be sterilised between batches (since they are porous and can therefore absorb all sorts of moulds).

Alternatively, you can also use smooth round stones as weights, but these need to be sterilised first. I scrub with washing detergent, boil for 30 minutes and then send them through the dishwasher and have never had spoilage issues. I dug them up from the garden. If this is just a step too far for you, feel free to put your stones in a ziplock freezer bag.

Another method of weighing down your veg in the jar is to use a plastic freezer bag filled with water; this is useful because it adapts to the shape of your jar. Otherwise you can use the plate and weight, the weight often being a glass or bottle. However, finding a plate small enough to fit inside many jars is fairly impossible. One solution is to use a round plastic lid, the sort that comes on peanut butter or ice-cream tubs. It needs to be food-grade plastic and should be sterilised or at least sent through the dishwasher before use. As these are flexible, you can fit them into all manner of storage jars and then weigh them down in the normal way using stones or a glass full of water.

SAUERKRAUT

There are many different ways to make kraut, but they all hold to the same principle of using salt and cabbage juice to get the lacto-fermentation started. I don't like overly salty kraut, but you may. Here lies the dark art; it takes practice to make your perfect kraut. You may not get there first time. You may need slightly more salt in warmer conditions than colder. Some people add a final layer of salt to the top, but if the juices are flowing, I think this is unnecessary and just makes for a very salty top layer. This is my tried-and-tested method and it has never failed me. The overnight step is unusual, but as I get consistent results I am not going to question it.

white cabbage
> *choose a firm, tightly packed variety such as Kilaton or Filderkraut (loose-leaf cabbage, like spring cabbage is harder to ferment)*

sea salt (never table salt)

knife or mandolin

large bowl or tub, for overnight salting

pestle, rolling pin or potato masher

sterilised pickling pot, stoneware crock or food-grade plastic container

tea-towel

weights (see page 102)

Shred your cabbage using either a mandolin or by finely slicing. Discard the very woody central core. You are aiming for 1mm slices; mine are rarely that thin, but it's nice to have something to aim for.

Place the cabbage in a large plastic tub or bowl – preferably something with a wide surface area – and pound it with a pestle or rolling pin (or a wine bottle if there's nothing else to hand). This will make the cabbage glisten, and this glistening is a sign that the cabbage is starting to release its juices. (This process needs to be more vigorous and lengthy if your cabbage is old or you have included any larger pieces.) Once your cabbage is glistening, sprinkle over a scant tablespoon of salt and cover with a damp tea-towel. Set aside at room temperature overnight. I was taught that this process draws out more liquid while exposing the kraut to good bacteria and yeasts in the air (it's the yeast that helps create the fine aroma of a good kraut). Who knows, something magic happens, though.

The next morning, you can start packing the cabbage into your pickling jar or crock – there is no need to rinse it first. You need to really press it down; any loose layer should reduce 50 per cent in volume. Every 10cm or so I add a teaspoon of sea salt. I use a pestle (or a potato masher) to pack the cabbage down. You should, after several layers, start to see lots of juice appearing. Eventually you

How to make the perfect pickling pot

The perfect pickling pot is made by Pickl-it in the US, but these lovely jars are far too expensive for me to import – so I DIYed my own version.

You will need a 1 litre Weck jar, a Weck jar plastic lid, a rubber bung (used for brewing), a bubble/airlock (also used for brewing) and a drill with a bit.

Drill a hole in the plastic Weck lid corresponding to the size of your rubber bung. Insert the bung and airlock. Place the plastic lid with the bung and airlock over the Weck jar and voilà – a foolproof pickling jar.

You can also use large Mason jars, although it's more difficult to drill through a metal lid and the lid may corrode over time. I've found Amazon as the best place to find Weck jars, lids and bungs.

Note: save the glass lid, clips and rubber ring from the Weck jar because you will need these to seal the jar after fermentation has finished.

I also purchased a number of sticker thermometers (used in home brewing and aquariums) that allow me to monitor the temperature of fermentation. These are not dishwasher proof and won't last, but at the beginning they'll give you a good idea of where in your kitchen is the best place to ferment.

want to get to a point where the juice covers the cabbage and there are no air bubbles. For a small-sized cabbage, I will use no more than 3 scant (not heaped) teaspoons of salt in packing. The general rule is for 10 pounds (4.5kg) of shredded cabbage you will need 6 tablespoons of salt. This ratio will turn the sugars in the cabbage to lactic acid.

After topping up with brine, you then need to weigh your cabbage down so that it sits under the brine. This is extremely important because if the kraut is exposed to air it will rot. There are many creative options, but my preferred method is to place a whole cabbage leaf on top and weigh it down with large stones (which I sterilise first). You can, particularly if flies are going to be a problem, cover with a tea-towel or lace doily. Lastly, sit the pot on a saucer – the first stages of fermentation can be messy and it might exude a lot of liquid.

Your cabbage now needs to be stored somewhere warm (18–22°C) for roughly 3–6 weeks (a lot depends on taste; in part you decide when you're happy with it). It can be cooler than this, but it will take longer to ferment. (I use sticker thermometers to monitor the temperature and these help me find the best place in my kitchen.)

Here the magic begins to happen. First it will bubble, perhaps considerably, then it will scum – you might even get a bloom of white mould (particularly if your pot doesn't have a lid). If you get mould, you should skim it off because it can lower the acid needed to ferment. Little bits of mould that are impossible to skim off can be stirred back into the cabbage; the lowering acid conditions will kill them off. However, if the conditions are too hot, and the brine begins to slime, you will end up with more mould than you can cope with. Sadly this means your kraut is no good and is only fit for the compost.

As long as there are bubbles, fermentation is happening. When they stop, which is usually at the point where the cabbage has reabsorbed much of its liquid (this tends to happen in week three), you have successfully fermented. Put a tight-fitting lid on your jar and store in a cool place at around 3°C, i.e. the fridge. You can waterbathe your kraut for long-term storage (see page 157) if you wish, but this will kill off all that is good and wholesome about it. Instead, I prefer to make small batches often and enjoy the wonders of the fermentation process again.

Variation
MAKING DIFFERENT FLAVOURED KRAUTS You can add all sorts of different flavours to kraut. Here are a few of my favourites: whole garlic cloves, peppercorns (pink look pretty in white cabbage), dill, caraway seeds (go easy, it's a powerful flavour, I wouldn't put more than a teaspoon in a 1 litre jar of kraut), sliced onion, pickling spices (mustard seeds, coriander), bay leaf or two, tart apples. And, of course, you can use red cabbage ('Rodeo' is good), which makes it rotkohl instead of sauerkraut.

On weights

I cannot stress enough how important it is to weigh down your kraut to stop it from becoming exposed to air. Remember: wherever there is air, the kraut will rot.

I use large stones that I dig up from the garden as weights. These I scrub with bicarbonate of soda, boil for 30 minutes and then send through the dishwasher on the hottest cycle. Once I am convinced that there's little dirt left, I use them to weigh down my pickles. They are free and, once clean, I have never had any contamination issues. If this freaks you out, I suggest you purchase some pastry weights (used for blind-baking pastry) and use these in a freezer bag to weigh down the cabbage.

Sauerkraut dos and don'ts

DO keep a record. Write down when you started your kraut and record any temperatures and variations, etc. A good method of monitoring the temperature is to use a sticker thermometer (used in home-brewing and aquariums). These are not dishwasher proof and won't last, but they should help you to find out where in your kitchen is the best place to ferment.

DO keep packing down the kraut every time you take some out; it needs to be permanently cosseted by its own juices.

DON'T mix batches or try to add fresh cabbage to existing kraut; it doesn't work.

DON'T eat your kraut if it smells or tastes bad; throw it on the compost.

Wash your hands before making kraut and keep all equipment, jars, pestles and plates, etc. clean at all times.

BIGOS STEW

This is one of my favourite recipes for cooked kraut. It tastes much better on day two or three, so make lots and enjoy the leftovers. This particular recipe is far from authentic I am afraid, but it is near enough to name so.

1 tablespoon olive oil

1 onion, sliced

a couple of garlic cloves, crushed

1 Kabanos Polish sausage, sliced into rounds 2cm or so thick

a couple of potatoes, peeled and diced *(optional, if you want to bulk out the meal)*

1 small cabbage (or similar quantity of kale)

300ml water or stock (*or vegetable water/ dried mushroom water, strained to remove those tiny grains of dirt*)

1 scant teaspoon hot paprika

2–3 glasses red wine

a handful of dried mushrooms, soaked

6 rashers of unsmoked bacon, cut into pieces

1 chorizo or spicy sausage, sliced into rounds 1cm or so thick

250g sauerkraut

salt and freshly ground black pepper

a handful of parsley, finely chopped

Heat the oil in a large casserole pan and sauté the onion, garlic and Kabanos sausage until everything is soft and golden. Add the potatoes, cabbage, water or stock, paprika, red wine and mushrooms and bring to the boil, stirring. Put on a tight-fitting lid and simmer gently for 45 minutes or so until you have a good stew.

In a separate pan, fry the bacon and the chorizo or spicy sausage, draining off the fat. Stir into the stew along with the kraut. Taste, add salt and pepper and a good handful of chopped parsley. Let the whole thing sit for several hours, reheat, eat, let it sit for another day or so and marvel as the flavours get better and better. Eat with crusty sourdough and more red wine.

PRESERVED LEMONS

I doubt that anyone has enough homegrown lemons to preserve, but preserved lemons are lovely with gremolata – which is an excellent way to preserve parsley and can be eaten with everything (see page 106). This is such a salty/acidic mixture that little can go wrong, and thus makes an ideal first fermenting project. This recipe was adapted from Casa Moro by Sam and Sam Clark.

4 washed lemons *(scrub hard if waxed)*
3 tablespoons sea salt
1 cinnamon stick
1 bay leaf
fresh or dried chilli, to taste
sterilised preserving jar with lid (see
    page 138)

Cut each lemon into quarters lengthways, keeping one end intact so that the lemon stays whole. Pack the salt into the lemons. You need to pack the lemons into a jar so that they begin to juice, then add the spices and weigh down so that the lemons don't float in their juices. This is very important, as exposed lemons won't ferment properly. Some people squeeze extra lemon juice over the lemons to ensure they aren't exposed.

Every other day gently shake the jar so that the juice and salt mix. After a week or so (depending on temperature) the liquid will become cloudy – this is natural. It takes roughly a month for the lemons to ferment. The liquid will thicken considerably during this time. Once the lemons are preserved, there's little chance of any bad bacteria entering them as long as you use clean tongs (or very clean fingers) to remove them. If they seem to be drying out squish them down into their juices again.

FLAVOURINGS You can flavour your preserved lemons in numerous ways. I like to include equal parts of toasted fennel, cumin and coriander seeds (about ¼ teaspoon each for 4 lemons), but many people use peppercorns.

Variation
PRESERVED LIMES These are preserved in exactly the same way as lemons, only using slightly more salt because they are not as acidic. Allow 1 tablespoon of salt per lime.

DRY-SALTED GREMOLATA

This is a bastardisation of a traditional method used to preserve dandelions, but you end up with a pretty good gremolata that is very good for seasoning all sorts of things – use on pork or fish, stuff in the belly of a roasting chicken or add to soups and pastas sauces (see page 191). Remember that it is incredibly salty and therefore you will not need any extra salt in your dish. If you want to make a less salty version, use fresh lemon rind instead of preserved lemons (but this will not keep as well). Once again, this follows the one-to-four rule: one part salt to four parts greens.

   1 preserved lemon (see page 105)
   2 garlic cloves
   300g flat-leaf parsley, washed and dried
   4 teaspoons coarse sea salt *(add an extra teaspoon of salt if not using a preserved lemon)*

Wash the preserved lemon really well to remove excess salt; remove the skin and finely chop, discarding the pith and flesh. Mince the garlic cloves and combine with the rest of the ingredients in a jar, cover with a tea-towel and set aside somewhere warm (the kitchen is fine) for 2–3 days, stirring occasionally. Transfer to a sterile container and store in a cool place (5–10°C is ideal). This will keep for several months.

DRY-SALTED GREENS

Greens – traditionally dandelions, parsley, chervil, rosemary, thyme and savory – can be preserved on a one-to-four rule with salt. These dry-salted herbs can then be used much like a stock cube, added to pasta sauces, soups, stews or used in vinaigrettes. Play around with a mix of herbs or keep the flavour separate. I find dry-salted parsley is very useful and keeps its vibrant green look and fresh taste for months.

   parsley (stems and leaves) *or greens of your choice, discarding any that are stringy or too woody*
sea salt

Roughly chop the parsley stems and leaves and weigh them. Measure out your salt, using a ratio of one part salt to four parts greens – so for 100g parsley you will need 25g salt.

   Combine the parsley and salt in a bowl or glass jar, cover with a tea-towel and set aside somewhere warm (the kitchen is fine) for 2–3 days, stirring occasionally. Transfer to a clean, sterile container and store in a cool place (5–10°C is ideal). This will keep for several months.

Variation

DRY-SALTED MIXED HERBS I often make a version using mixed fresh herbs, which forms a good basis for flavouring stocks, etc. Leeks can also be used. Bear in mind that the herbs will be very salty, so go easy on the seasoning when cooking.

DRY-SALTED SALAMOIA BOLOGNESE

This traditional seasoning from Bologna has many variations – some versions contain basil, others include lemon zest or black pepper – but the basic recipe remains the same. Basically, you need lots of salt to keep everything preserved. The herbs and garlic must be fresh; this is essential, as the flavours just don't work with dried herbs. This version was given to me by Paolo Arrigo, but I also make it with equal parts rosemary and sage.

Salamoia Bolognese is a storecupboard essential. It can be used in pasta sauces, on eggs, with fish, potatoes or on grilled vegetables – wherever you might want salt, try this as a substitute.

> 10g rosemary leaves
> 5g sage leaves
> 1 large garlic clove, peeled
>   *(you can add more if you wish)*
> 100g coarse sea salt

Chop the herbs very finely; it is often easier to do this in stages. Once they are chopped nice and fine, add in the garlic and keep chopping until you have a fine herb and garlic paste. Scrape the mixture into a bowl and stir in the sea salt. Spoon into an airtight container and store somewhere cool and dark. It should keep for at least 4 months.

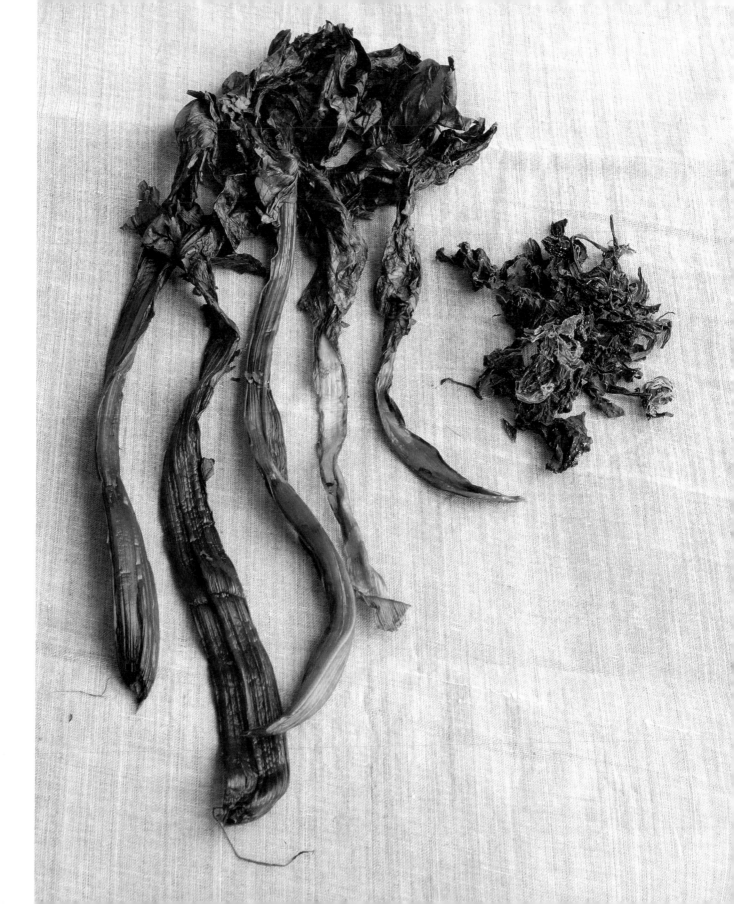

If you worship at the Church of Fermentation then at some point you must read Sandor Katz' seminal works *Wild Fermentation* and *The Art of Fermentation*, both of which are full of wonderful and weird flavours. I learnt to make Gundruk, a Nepalese traditional fermented green, the Katz way but have adapted it to suit our less than sunny summers.

Gundruk is a truly funky flavour. Pungent, like a good kraut, but supersour. I personally can't get enough of the raw stuff, but it's perhaps one for the truly converted.

GUNDRUK USING SWISS CHARD OR KALE

I have given instructions for making both fresh Gundruk and dried below. I use the fresh stuff as a condiment for flavouring rice, fish and chicken dishes, and the dried version in stocks and soups (much like a soup cube). Alternatively, you could rehydrate the dried version and fry it lightly with potatoes much like you would Saag Aloo.

> a carrier bag of greens (stems and all)
> 1 x 250ml sterilised glass storage jar with
>   a lid, a jam jar is perfect
> sunlight or a temperature of 18–21°C

Wash the greens and leave them outside on a baking tray in the sun (or in a warm kitchen) to wilt. Do not cover them, as it is very important that they are exposed to natural yeasts in the air.

Once your greens are limp, run a rolling pin over them a couple of times until they release some juices. At this point, you can start to pack them into your storage jar. Pack them in tightly, as you would kraut, and use the end of a rolling pin or a pestle to press down firmly. The idea is to get all those greens to fit into the jar. You need a lot pressure, but not so much that you totally mush the greens. Miraculously, just like sauerkraut, the greens will start to release a lot of liquid and will quickly become submerged in their own juices.

Once the jar is full, cover with a lid. Place it somewhere warm, such as on a sunny windowsill, for 2–3 weeks; I sometimes sit mine on top of my dehydrator while it is running or on top of the stove. It could bubble a lot, so it might be a good idea to put a saucer underneath to catch any juices. After a while, just like sauerkraut, it will stop bubbling and start to reabsorb its own juices; this means it is ready. It will look remarkably like seaweed.

You have two choices. Either take out a few stems at a time, chop finely and use as a condiment for rice, fish or chicken dishes, or take the more traditional route and dry your Gundruk for long-term storage. Do this either in a very low oven (60°C) or dehydrator (or, if the weather allows, out on the washing line) dry the gundruk until it is brittle. This will take 4–6 hours. It must be completely dry or it will mould. Don't worry about any white bloom; this is just the natural yeast drying out.

TORSHI LIFT-PICKLED TURNIPS

Torshi is the name for many Middle Eastern and even Eastern European pickles eaten with mezze or at the end of a meal. My favourite way to eat them is in a falafel sandwich. It dyes the turnips a deep pink all the way through, it's a pretty spectacular pickle. The principles are a short ferment (only 2 weeks), with the addition of some sort of acid (although some versions omit this).

Many recipes are made with white wine vinegar, but I prefer the more subtle flavour of lemon juice. (If you prefer to use vinegar, follow the recipe but substitute the lemon juice for 125ml white wine vinegar and reduce the water to 500ml.)

45g sea salt
750ml water
3–4 medium-sized turnips *(no larger than the size of a tennis ball)*
3–4 garlic cloves
1–2 small beetroots or 1 large beetroot
a few celery leaves (optional)
juice of 1 lemon
sterilised pickling jar *(preferably a perfect pickling pot, see page 99)*

Dissolve the salt in the water to create a brine and alllow to coll.

Wash and scrub the turnips and cut into slices 1–2cm thick; they look prettiest if all the slices are even, like half moons. Peel the garlic and score for a more pronounced garlic flavour (or leave whole if you don't want this). Peel the beetroots and cut into quarters; the more you cut the beetroot, the more it will bleed, turning the turnip from pink to dark red.

Pack the jar with alternating layers of turnip, garlic, beetroot and celery leaves (if using). If you want your pickle to be light pink, place the beetroots on top.

Add the lemon juice to the brine and pour over the vegetables. The vegetables must be fully submerged in the brine, so you may need to weigh them down with stones or similar (see page 102) to keep them covered and stop them floating to the top.

Seal the jar and set aside in a warm place (18-22 °C) for no more than 2 weeks, swirling to distribute the colour every once in a while.

After 2 weeks, move your jar to the fridge, where the pickle will keep for up to 6 weeks. You can store them for longer, but they will begin to lose their crispness.

Kimchi is an ancient pickle made using a method that is over 2,000 years old. It is thought to have originated in China around 12BC as a technique for preserving out of season greens using salt. Kimchi was brought to Korea in around AD37 but it wasn't until the 16th century that preserving cabbage with red chillies became popular. There are now over 200 kimchi recipes and no Korean meal is complete without some kimchi.

Kimchi kicks its way to your taste buds, it hollers out its heat and assaults your senses, but once you've got over the shock of such a strong flavour you are left wanting more. I remember the first time I tasted kimchi. It was with a fellow student called Paul (actually that wasn't his name; halfway through the course he informed us that he just chose it so he'd fit in better!). Anyway, Paul took me out for lunch to sample his traditional cuisine. I was hooked instantly and still eat at the same restaurant whenever I can to sample the many kimchis it produces.

WHAT IS KIMCHI? Kimchi is a traditional method of preserving different winter vegetables using salt. There are two basic categories of kimchi: seasonal *kimchim,* highlighting an ingredient that is fresh and readily available at any given moment, and stored kimchi, *kimjang,* for winter use. Kimchi is usually served as a side dish alongside bland rice, but it can also be used in soups and stews; my favourite way of serving kimchi is in pancakes (see page 117), a quick, cheap and hugely satisfying meal for a cold winter's night.

The tenants of this fermentation are red chilli peppers, salt, garlic, ginger and fermented fish sauce. Some recipes call for a starch in the form of rice flour to bind the ingredients together. The fermented fish sauce is responsible for kimchi's unique smell and taste. This is traditionally made from baby shrimp, anchovies or corvine (complete with its intestines), which are salted and left to ferment. During the fermentation process the protein is broken down into amino acids (hence the delightful smell), which further promotes fermentation in the vegetables.

NUTRITIONAL BENEFITS OF KIMCHI Kimchi is packed with a huge range of vitamins that are invaluable during cold Korean winters, especially when fresh vegetables can be unavailable. It is particularly rich in B vitamins, as well as containing protein from the fish sauce. It is very good for your digestive system and it is said that Koreans eat so much kimchi that without it they can't digest properly.

It is worth noting that after a long search I still can't find anyone who's got food poisoning from kimchi. A Korean study found that the good bacteria in kimchi can kill off bad bacteria such as salmonella, found in meat and fish. So, it truly is good for you.

UNDERSTANDING KIMCHI I have read several books on kimchi, including Lee and Lee's *Kimchi – A Korean Health Food* (a wonderful technicolour tour of kimchi with often baffling translations), but cannot claim that my recipes are even a close approximation of what is obviously a fine art.

The Koreans take their kimchi seriously. They even have public holidays for the winter kimchi-making ceremony, called *kimjang*, when neighbours, families and friends get together to make huge amounts of kimchi. Every region has its own variation – some are made with radishes, others with Chinese cabbage or fruit – and each has its own precise style of cutting and presentation. Kimchi truly is an art form that one day I would love to master. In the meantime, I shall carry on with my strange experiments.

SOURCING OR GROWING THE INGREDIENTS FOR KIMCHI Fermented fish sauce is an essential ingredient that can be hard to come by in the UK, unless you happen to live next to a Korean store. Make sure

you find a product that is intended for kimchi, as many regular fish sauces contain preservatives that will ruin the natural fermentation process. If you cannot get hold of Korean fish sauce (or any other preservative-free brand), you could make a less authentic, but still acceptable, fish-free version.

Korean red pepper is used to create the distinct taste and colour of kimchi. A native red chilli, which is very hot, is usually mixed with a Chinese red pepper, which is larger and milder with thicker skin, essentially for getting that bright red colour. These are sun dried and ground into a fine powder or, for certain kimchis, are cut into thin strips and dried.

If you are making kimchi from chillies you have grown yourself, mix and match a few different varieties until you end up with a spicy, bright red powder. If you don't have enough dried chillies or can't get hold of Korean chili powder, try adding some unsmoked paprika with the chilli powder – I've tried this before and it seems to achieve the right flavour; it is a compromise, but it's as close as you can get to the real stuff.

There is a wide choice of greens available to choose from. Indian mustard greens are traditionally used, but these can be difficult to source in the UK. I have had successful results with Oriental mustard greens I grow from seed. Try 'Golden Streaks' for a mild mustard flavour, or 'Giant Red' for more heat (this works well with radish). Watercress is often added because it is rich in vitamins A, C and calcium. This is easy to grow yourself in a bucket; alternatively, substitute American landcress.

One of the most popular and widely recognisable kimchis is made with Chinese cabbage. However, I find it very hard to grow organically at home – it requires steady temperatures, a lot of water and no slugs – so I tend to omit it from my recipes.

Radish is an incredibly popular ingredient, and thankfully I am very good at growing radishes. Many dishes call for ponytail radish, which is a white Asian radish with a round end. If you can get hold of the seeds, I suggest growing some specifically to ferment.

ROOT VEGETABLE KIMCHI

(adapted from Sandor Katz's Wild Fermentation*)*

2 turnips

2 Jerusalem artichokes

2 mooli radishes

2 carrots

4 spring onions

a small bunch of garlic chives

a bunch of watercress (or landcress)

a small bunch of mustard greens

FOR THE CHILLI/ GINGER/ GARLIC PASTE

4 garlic cloves, peeled and crushed

1 x 5cm piece of root ginger, peeled
   and grated

3 teaspoons red chilli powder made into a
   paste with a little water *(you can add a
   lot more if you wish)*

Korean fish sauce *(must be preservative
   free)*, to taste

pickling jar *(preferably a perfect pickling
   pot, see page 99)*

A traditional recipe I have calls for a 15 per cent brine (150g salt dissolved in 1 litre of water or for this recipe 75g in 500ml). This is a lot of salt. If you wish to use less, use 10% (10g in 1 litre of water) or,

---

The key to kimchi success

\# Always make small batches of kimchi. Large jars of kimchi aren't easy to store. If you keep opening the jar and disturbing the contents this can encourage further fermentation, which will turn your kimchi into something truly horrid in a matter of hours.

\# The ideal temperature for fermenting is 14°C, which is considerably cooler than the temperature you ferment sauerkraut.

\# Once fermented, kimchi should be stored somewhere cool between 2 and 10°C.

\# If your kimchi is slimy, mouldy or smells bad (I mean 'bad' not strong), please throw it away.

---

for this recipe, 5g in 500ml. Dissolve the salt in the water over heat if necessary and allow to cool.

Wash, peel and cut the root vegetables into 5cm pieces; do the same with the greens. Add to the brine mixture and set aside for 3–4 hours to soften.

Once the vegetables have softened slightly, rinse them really well in fresh water and taste them. They should taste salty, but in a pleasant way; if they taste distinctly unsalty, pop them back in the brine for a further hour. Rinse well, reserving the brine for later.

Cut the softened vegetables into thin, bite-sized pieces – anything from a couple of centimetres thick to the size of a matchstick. The idea here is to make them all the same size so you don't end up with a huge mouthful of just one vegetable. Place the vegetables in a large bowl.

Prepare the spices by mixing the garlic, ginger and chilli powder into a thick paste. At this point, if you have some Korean fish sauce add a dash or two. Add the spice mixture to the vegetables and combine really well with your (clean) hands to coat them evenly on all sides.

Place the vegetables into a sterilised jar, pressing them down firmly as you go. You should start to see some liquid rise in the jar, which will increase over the next few days. If you don't get any brine, add 3 per cent brine solution (see page 97).

Weigh the vegetables down so they are fully submerged in the brine, topping up with more brine if necessary. I use clean scrubbed stones as weights, but you could use a ziplock bag filled with water (see page 98).

Place the kimchi in a warm place (14°C). After three days it will start to ferment (and may bubble a bit so place a saucer under your pot as it can bubble over). It is very important that the kimchi doesn't ferment at higher temperatures because it will quickly spoil. Once it tastes good (usually a lot of the brine has become reabsorbed at this point), transfer to the fridge at 2–5°C, where it will keep for a further month – hell, I've eaten it after 3–4 months, but let's be on the safe side.

PUMPKIN KIMCHI

½ pumpkin, peeled, deseeded and diced
    into 2cm chunks

coarse sea salt

6 radishes *(I use 'Spanish Black Round')*
    or 1 large mooli, cut into rounds 2cm
    thick, including any leaves

a small bunch of mustard greens *(I use
    'Golden Streaks' for its mild flavour)*

a small bunch of watercress/landcress

4 large garlic cloves, peeled and crushed

2 heaped teaspoons Korean red pepper
    powder *(or a mixture of chilli and
    unsmoked paprika, see page 113)*, or
    to taste

1 x 5cm piece of root ginger, peeled
    and grated

4 spring onions cut into 5cm lengths

sterilised pickling jar *(preferably a
    perfect pickling pot, see page 99)*

Sprinkle the pumpkin and radish with a little salt and set aside for 3–4 hours until softened,

Soak the radish leaves, mustard leaves and watercress/landcress in the brine solution of 3% (30g in 1 litre) until soft; rinse and cut into 5cm lengths.

Combine the garlic, red pepper powder and ginger to make a paste. Splash a little water in if necessary.

Place the pumpkin, radishes, greens and spring onions in a bowl and mix in the red pepper paste, using your hands to coat the vegetables thoroughly all over.

Pack the vegetables in a pickling jar, add weights and set aside to ferment at 14°C. After three days it should start to ferment and bubble a bit (place a saucer underneath to collect any escaping juices). After a week it should have fermented. Once fermented, store in an airtight container in the fridge at 2–5°C.

LEAFY GREEN KIMCHI

This kimchi is a great way to use up radish leaves. For best results, pick off the younger leaves of regular radishes, discarding any tougher leaves, or find a variety grown specially for leaf use, such as leaf radish 'Sai Sai', 'Hong Vit' or 'Red Stemmed' with less hairy leaves.

200g radish leaves (or other mild oriental
    leaf such as mizuna)

coarse sea salt

3 garlic cloves, peeled and crushed

1 small piece of root ginger, peeled and
    grated (5cm)

3 teaspoons Korean red pepper powder,
    or to taste

1 tablespoon rice flour *(or plain if you
    can't get rice)*

2 teaspoons sesame seeds, briefly toasted
    in a dry frying pan to release their
    fragrance

4 spring onions, cut into 5cm lengths

a sterilised jar *(preferably a perfect
    pickling pot, see page 99)*

Wash the radish leaves and cut them into 5cm lengths. Sprinkle with salt and set aside to soften for an hour or so. Taste, and if the leaves taste unpleasantly salty, rinse.

Combine the garlic, ginger, red pepper powder and rice flour with a little water to make a paste. Stir in the toasted sesame seeds.

Place the radish leaves in a bowl with the spring onions and red pepper paste and mix thoroughly with your hands. Pack the mixture into your pickling pot and weigh it down with stones or similar (see page 102) so that the greens sit in their own juices. Set aside to ferment at 14°C. After 3 days it should start to ferment; try a little and leave longer if you'd like a stronger flavour. Once fermented, seal and store at 10°C; it should keep for up to a month.

Lazy kimchi dining

KIMCHI EGG-FRIED RICE

Serves 1
1 tablespoon sunflower oil
1 portion cooked rice *(at my laziest I use that precooked rice in a pouch)*
3 tablespoons homemade kimchi of your choice, cut into smaller pieces if you'd prefer, plus some kimchi juice
a handful of peas, pea shoots, watercress/ landcress or spring onions (or some other quick-frying green)
1 egg, beaten
soy sauce, to taste

Heat the oil in a wok or frying pan, add the rice and start to fry. Add the kimchi and juice and stir-fry over a high heat until it starts to steam a little. Add the greens and stir-fry rapidly to heat them through, then crack in the egg. Whip it around to create egg-fried rice and serve. Season to taste with soy sauce, but remember the kimchi is naturally salty so go easy. If your kimchi is as spicy as mine, you might need to keep a jug of cold water handy when you devour it.

KIMCHI RAMEN

This is a trashy meal, but hell, that's what a hangover is for. And at least the kimchi is good for you.

450ml water
4 tablespoons homemade kimchi of your choice
1 packet instant ramen noodles, plus the sachet of soup stock
2 spring onions, cut into 5cm lengths
1 small hot red chilli , finely chopped (optional)
1 egg

Bring the water to the boil, drop in the kimchi and simmer for 5 minutes. Add the soup stock and ramen noodles and cook until they are done. Throw in the spring onions and chilli. Carefully crack in the egg and simmer gently until it is softly poached. Taste and season with a little salt if necessary.

KIMCHI PANCAKES

These pancakes are thicker than French crepes but not quite as thick as an American-style pancake. You could add toasted black sesame seeds, chive flowers and a dash of soy sauce for variety.

Makes 2 large pancakes
FOR THE FILLING
2 tablespoons homemade kimchi of your choice *(traditionally cabbage kimchi is used, but I've used all sorts)*; slice the kimchi up if it's too bulky.
2 bacon rashers, fat trimmed off, cut into thin strips and marinated in a little soy sauce, sesame oil and grated root ginger (optional)
OR a little Korean pickled wild garlic (see page 81), as a vegetarian option
1 large spring onion, cut into 5cm lengths
FOR THE PANCAKE BATTER
90g plain flour (or gluten-free rice flour)
120ml water
1 small egg, beaten with a pinch of salt
sunflower oil, for frying

Make up the pancake batter by sifting the flour into a bowl and gradually whisking in the water and beaten egg until smooth.

Heat the oil over a high heat in a frying pan and fry the bacon, draining off any excess fat. Ladle in half the pancake batter and tilt the pan so it spreads to fill the pan and the bottom just starts to set a little. Arrange the kimchi, bacon (or wild garlic) and spring onion on the pancake and cook over a low heat until the base is golden brown and the top has just set (use a lid if necessary).

SOUR DILL PICKLES

This is another fermenting classic. These are those sour, salty gherkins that you get in an American deli, perfect with a Reuben sandwich and a cold beer. Sour dill pickles are one of the highlights of my pickling year.

This recipe works best if you use gherkin-type cucumbers, or at least very small cukes. You will find many recipes for quick dill pickles that substitute the lacto-fermentation with vinegar, which is fine I guess if you are pushed for time, but I find a long fermentation really makes the tang.

If you wish, you could substitute the cucumbers for French beans to make fermented dilly bean pickle; if you do this, omit the mustard seeds.

This recipe is for a small batch of cucumbers that will fit inside a pickling pot. I've often found those large batch recipes intimidating, particularly if you are not sure of the process. Try it, like it, scale it up.

Many traditional recipes for sour dill pickles call for a 24- or 48-hour ferment, after which time the cucumbers are rinsed and stored in sweetened vinegar for long-term storage. To me this kills off all the fun (and the goodness) of the natural fermentation process. This recipe takes 1–4 weeks to ferment.

coarse sea salt

500g pickling cucumbers such as 'Parisian Pickling' *(i.e. small gherkin-like cucumbers no more than 10cm long)*

3 garlic cloves, peeled and scored

FOR THE FLAVOURINGS

2 heads of flowering dill (or 2 tablespoons chopped dill leaves and ¼ teaspoon dill seeds)

¼ teaspoon mustard seeds

¼ teaspoon black peppercorns

1 small bay leaf

½ small fresh red chilli, sliced (optional)

1 grape leaf (see page 84)

1 litre sterilised pickling jar *(preferably a perfect pickling pot, see page 99)*

Make up a brine solution by dissolving 40g salt in 500ml water (8 per cent brine solution). Stir until all the salt is dissolved. Wash the cukes, gently removing any blossom remaining on the bottom.

Place the herbs and spices at the bottom of your pickling jar, and then gently tip the jar on its side and pack in the cucumbers and garlic. By placing the jar sideways, you are able to get an even stack, otherwise your cucumbers will end up topsy-turvy. Pour the brine over the cucumbers so they are submerged.

Place the grape leaf on top of the jar and weigh down the cucumbers with clean stones or similar (see page 102). This is important; the cucumbers must be fully submerged in the brine or they will rot.

Cover the jar with a clean cloth or your perfect pickling pot lid.

There are several options for fermenting. If you have fermented in a standard glass jar (with no airlock), put your cucumbers somewhere cool and bright (but not in direct sunlight), as the sunlight should slow down the formation of any surface scum. If you are using a perfect pickling pot or similar, place in a similar spot. The length of time your pickles take to ferment will depend on the temperature. As I said before, I favour a slow ferment at a lower temperature (16–21°C); this takes around 4 weeks. If you are fermenting at higher temperatures (18–21°C) your ferment should be ready in 1–2 weeks.

Check the jar every day. If mould appears (hugely unlikely in a perfect pickling pot), skim it off as best you can and then stir the jar to disperse any smaller particles of mould; the acidic conditions in the brine should soon kill them off. If necessary, wash your lids and weights if they become mouldy.

After a week, try the pickle. If it is pickled to perfection, put on an airtight lid and move it to a cooler spot (such as a fridge or cellar). If your pickle is not sour enough (i.e. if you are fermenting in cooler conditions), leave it for a bit longer.

Store your dill cucumbers in an airtight container at 10–16°C. They should keep for up to 3 months.

TABASCO

Tabasco sauce is made from Tabasco chillies, Capsicum frutescens 'Tabasco', which are named after the Mexican state. However, you can make a perfectly good version of this famous hot sauce using any hot chilli. The secret to a good hot sauce is a long ferment. Apparently, true Tabasco sauce is aged for up to 3 years in oak barrels. This recipe is rushed in comparison, but makes a lovely sauce and you can make it as mild or as hot as you like.

**30 small red chillies or 15 larger-style
   chillies
salt
white wine vinegar
sterilised storage jar** (*preferably a perfect
   pickling pot, see page 99*)

Wash the chillies and remove the stems. Finely chop the flesh and seeds or blend to a paste in a food-processor – this is the sensible option, as chopping will leave you with fiery fingers. Weigh your chilli paste and work out how much salt you will need. The ratio should be 30 parts chilli to 1 part salt.

Scoop the mixture into your storage jar and stir in the salt. Cover with a tea-towel (or your perfect pickling pot lid) and set aside in a cool place somewhere between 18 and 21°C for 24 hours.

After 24 hours you will notice the salt has started to draw moisture out of the chillies. It is very important that the chilli paste remains submerged in this briny solution throughout the fermentation process; if the chillies are exposed to air, bad organisms will get in and ruin the fermentation process. If there is not enough briny liquid to cover your chillies, then add a teaspoon of salt and stir it in well and set aside for a further 1–2 hours. After this time, the briny liquid will start to separate just a little from the chilli pulp and form a layer. This thin layer is all you need to keep your chillies submerged. You may find that you still get a white mould, which you will have to skim off regularly.

I find that stirring the mixture once a week can stop this from happening.

The fermentation process will take about 4 weeks at 18–21°C. You can ferment at lower temperatures than this, but the process will take longer, up to 3 months.

After 4 weeks, you need to add the vinegar. Do this bit by bit, tasting as you go until you get that distinct fiery acidic flavour (don't add too much or your sauce will be too watery). Set aside for a further week to allow the flavours to blend before tasting again. Add a little more vinegar if necessary.

The final step is to strain your sauce through a sieve lined with several layers of muslin. You can leave in a fair amount of pulp if you wish, but I wouldn't recommend leaving the seeds in.

Store in an airtight bottle in the fridge. This sauce should keep for several months, longer perhaps – but I wouldn't know because it goes quickly in my house!

TSUKEMONO

These are those delightfully bright-coloured Japanese pickles that you find in bento boxes, the ones that are brought to any and every Japanese meal. These quick pickles are not for long-term storage. There are numerous methods for single-day pickling, but I've concentrated here on the bizarre and wonderful nukazuke pickles that are fermented in a rice bran bed called a nukadoko.

Creating a nuka-bed is not a project. It is a relationship with your pickles, one entirely built on consistent love. If you relished a 30-day ferment of Tabasco, thought kimchi was a walk in the park, if you keep a sourdough starter or have made a beer or kombucha, this project is for you – it might even make you ridiculously happy.

In Japan, a well-made nuka-bed is handed down from one generation to the next. Imagine inheriting your grandmother's pickling pot with the same culture she inherited off her grandmother? If the thought of daily attending to a bed of wet, fermenting bran is, as Simon the photographer put it, 'like cleaning out a drain' every day, then perhaps you should just head to your Japanese restaurant and realise that those tiny aubergines and finely cut pickled daikon have been produced for your dining pleasure with a lot of love. Either that, or persuade someone from Japan to bring you back some instant nuka (sold as nukazuke no moto in a bag or nukadoko in a plastic bucket).

Here's the first thing you should know about your nuka-bed. It has to be turned, by hand, EVERY DAY. That means when you go on holiday you either have to entrust your nuka-bed to someone or take it with you.

You may have to order the rice bran online. I have read that you can substitute the rice bran for wheat bran or even cornflakes, but I've never tried them out.

Your nuka-bed will smell strange, not unpleasant by any means, but I can imagine the smell might not be for everyone. And yes, Simon is right, it is a bit like putting your hand down a blocked drain – but the pickles are amazing. The lactobacillus that inhabits the bran ferments the pickles; the brine added to the bran helps to create the right environment; the bread and eggshells encourage the right yeast; and the spices, seaweeds, peels and other vegetables give the bed a unique flavour. No two nuka-beds are alike; each will produce its own unique, subtle flavour. Some beds call for beer or sake to introduce different yeasts. I've added dried Gundruk to my bed to help increase the yeast count. It definitely gets the fermenting going quickly in a new bed.

You may find, particularly in hotter weather, that you get a white mould (not too dissimilar to the mould you may get on krauts) on top of the bed. This is an indicator that the mixture is a little too wet, slightly underfed and that bad bacteria are starting to move in. Add more rice bran and stir more frequently. Stirring the bed helps to oxygenate the yeast, preventing the undesirable anaerobic bacteria from moving in. On very hot days, say above 30°C, you may have to stir twice a day.

If your bed is too wet and you don't have bran, you could add dried beans (dried soya beans are traditionally used in Japan) to absorb the moisture; they will also impart a subtle flavour.

Both dried chilies and fresh garlic are used to stop overfermentation and to keep pests out of the bran (I'm guessing that could be a problem when your bran is decades old!). I hope to never find any worms in my bran.

If it smells sour or just plain wrong, dump it on the compost and start again.

If you want to put your bed to rest for a while because you no longer want to pickle, you can store it in the fridge (if necessary, in a plastic freezer bag, if your pickling pot doesn't fit). Remember you will still need to keep turning it, just less frequently. If you want to go away (or just stop turning it every day), you can store it for a month in the fridge. You can also store the mash in the freezer if you want to take a longer break.

5 strips 'kombu' seaweed, each 10cm long
    and 2–3cm wide
3 egg shells
2 slices sourdough bread, sliced, cubed
    and soaked in water to form a mush
brine solution made by dissolving 85g salt
    in 1 litre water
125g miso paste
1kg rice bran *(available from health food
    shops)*
1 x 2.5cm piece of root ginger, grated
1–2 dried red chillies, crushed
peel of 1 apple, dried slightly to sweeten it
    (optional)
1 garlic clove, peeled but left whole
1 small cabbage or some turnip leaves
    *(these are essential, to get your
    ferment going)*
assorted seasonal vegetables of your
    choice – *e.g. pickling cucumbers,
    radishes, aubergines, peas, beans,
    young courgettes, carrots, turnips or
    Jerusalem artichokes – these are
    added from day 8 onwards*
a pickling pot – *I use a stone pickling pot,
    but a plastic tub is fine*

DAY 1. Rehydrate the seaweed: place it in a bowl, cover with warm water and set aside for 30 minutes; drain, saving the water. Strain the water through a sieve to remove any grit and set aside.

Wash and crush the egg shells and make up the brine. (It may be easiest to dissolve the salt in hot water – if so, let the brine cool to handling temperature before adding it to the bran.) Dissolve the miso paste in the reserved seaweed water.

Place the bran, bread, egg shells, seaweed, ginger, chillies and miso mixture in a large saucepan. Slowly pour in the brine, stirring with a wooden spoon so there are no dry patches. The bran should feel like wet sand – moist, but not swimming in the brine.

Scoop the mixture into your crock and add the first of the vegetables – such as a cabbage leaf or the core even, or a few turnip leaves. Bury them deep within the bran, making sure they do not touch. Set aside somewhere cool, at room temperature for 24 hours.

DAY 2. Turn your bed using clean hands (not a spoon), remove the old cabbage core or turnip leaves and put in some fresh cabbage or turnip leaves. The reason you use your hands is because much of the yeast that encourages the ferment comes from your skin; if this grosses you out, perhaps a nuka-bed is not for you! The rest will come from the fresh vegetables you place in the pot every day.

Some recipes advise weighing the bran down so that it sits in brine. I have not found this necessary. However, I have found that after a day two it may be necessary to top up with more brine if the mixture is not moist to touch. (You will need to make up a fresh solution for this by dissolving 15g salt in 250ml water.) If it looks like you have too much liquid, press a saucer into the top of the bran and draw off any excess, or alternatively add a little more bran.

DAYS 3–7 Turn your bed EVERY DAY using clean hands. Take out the old cabbage/turnip leaves and put in some fresh cabbage or turnip leaves.

Towards the end of the first week, you should start to notice that the cabbage leaves are starting to turn a slightly different colour and they are becoming limp, but still with a bit of crunch. This means the ferment is working. By the end of the week, be brave and taste one of the leaves. It should have a slightly sour taste, salty and distinctly pickled. If this isn't the case, carry on turning your bed and replacing the leaves daily for a further week up to 3 weeks in total.

FROM DAY 8 ONWARDS Once the fermentation process has started, you can start pickling your seasonal vegetables. The vegetables need to be clean, but are best, I've found, left whole. It seems to work best if you use small vegetables, aubergines that are about 10cm long, a similar size for cucumbers and carrots. Turnips and radishes should be gobstopper sized and left whole, but it's worth experimenting.

Bury your prepared vegetables a few at a time, in the bran mixture, making sure that they don't touch. Fermentation times will vary, according to the size of your vegetables and the temperature of your room, but I would advise somewhere between 1 and 2 days. (You can leave radishes for as long as a month, but they end up quite a peculiar flavour!) REMEMBER YOU MUST TURN YOUR BED EVERY DAY WITH CLEAN HANDS.

Periodically, you will have to top up your bed with more brine, bran, ginger, seaweed, miso or beer. Add a little at a time. A good indicator that it's time to add new ingredients is when the seaweed has completely dissolved in the bed.

ON SUGAR

jams, jellies and cheeses

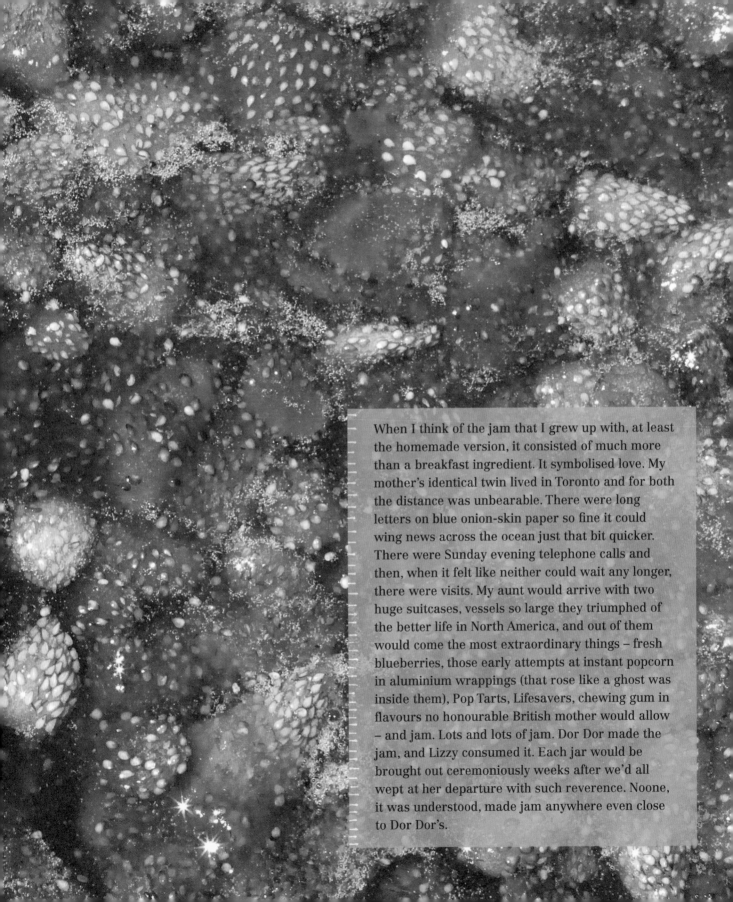

When I think of the jam that I grew up with, at least the homemade version, it consisted of much more than a breakfast ingredient. It symbolised love. My mother's identical twin lived in Toronto and for both the distance was unbearable. There were long letters on blue onion-skin paper so fine it could wing news across the ocean just that bit quicker. There were Sunday evening telephone calls and then, when it felt like neither could wait any longer, there were visits. My aunt would arrive with two huge suitcases, vessels so large they triumphed of the better life in North America, and out of them would come the most extraordinary things – fresh blueberries, those early attempts at instant popcorn in aluminium wrappings (that rose like a ghost was inside them), Pop Tarts, Lifesavers, chewing gum in flavours no honourable British mother would allow – and jam. Lots and lots of jam. Dor Dor made the jam, and Lizzy consumed it. Each jar would be brought out ceremoniously weeks after we'd all wept at her departure with such reverence. Noone, it was understood, made jam anywhere even close to Dor Dor's.

That is, except my other aunt, who was French, and thus put a different spin on the process. An active member of Greenpeace, Amnesty International and once chained to Greenham Common (about the same time as my memory tells me the jars first started appearing in our house), her jars were, and still are, a political event. They are named after whatever political injustice is bothering her at the time she makes them – and sometimes after a celebration of justice – the idea being that something so significant as injustice, poverty and war would instantly tell the eater when the jam was made. When I was younger, her jam names often seemed completely obscure (at least to me). Now I can't imagine not naming a jam after an event, though not all of mine are quite so politically minded.

Here was my education in jam. School may have fed me on mass-produced stuff, but home taught me that jam was jewel coloured, rich, sweet or bitter, that it could skate across the butter or stand firm with it leaving teeth marks as a testament. I still, every now and again, crave cheap white bread, just-so-softened butter and my mother's greengage jam that tingled when it hit the roof of your mouth.

You could leave cartoon-like bites in that combination, the jam being of stronger stuff than the bread.

A good jam should sing with the flavour of its fruit and in order for this to happen it must simmer first and boil to set, never the other way round. The best jam is allowed to release its flavour first by macerating in its own juices. If you can, chop the fruit the night before and add part (if not all) of the sugar needed plus any herbs or spices and leave it to mingle, stirring occasionally so that the sugar dissolves. It may be necessary to strain the fruit and herbs overnight if you want a clear jelly, otherwise after a night of all the ingredients getting to know each other, add extra sugar if needed and start to simmer.

Of course you might not have time for an overnight sugar soak. Don't worry, good jam can still be made from more traditional methods. I think my best word of advice is not to make huge batches, just a little batch here and there to ring the changes with the seasons. A good homemade jam made well does not have to be just about bread and butter – made with the right spices, it can be just as good with goat's cheese or with meat.

How jam is preserved

It's all about the sugar with jam: the more sugar you add, the longer the jam lasts. However, tread warily because too much sugar will make your jam sticky and sickly.

The sugar's trick is to lock up the available amount of water in the fruit, thus hiding it away from spoilage organisms. This, along with heat, the right amount of acid in the fruit and the lack of oxygen in the jar, serves to preserve your fruit. After drying, jam-making is perhaps one of the easiest and most rewarding ways to preserve a harvest. In no time, you can go from inexperienced to creating your own masterpieces.

After a while you will start to be horrified by how much sugar you use; older recipes in particular call for mountains of the stuff (or at least pound for pint – that is, an equal measure of fruit and sugar). However, it is entirely possible to remove a great deal of sugar by employing pectin to do the setting.

Commercial pectin is expensive and often demands that you use just as much sugar. However, homemade pectin (see page 130), made at the beginning of the season, is pretty much free and it's a joy to work with. These jams don't store for the year or more that your grandmother's might have, but who wants yesterday's jam when there's tomorrow's to be had?

Meet the jam family

Depending on where you call home, there is more than just jam. Jellies, preserves, conserves, marmalades, butter and cheese are all methods of preserving fruit.

JAMS are made from whole fruit, either mashed, cut or macerated, added to sugar and sometimes pectin (you won't find pectin in recipes dating from World War II). Jam should be set, but not firm, and have no free liquid; you should not be able to see the spoon's impression in the jam pot. Jam should also be brightly coloured.

JELLIES are made from the clear juices of fruit. They should be firm enough to be turned out of the pot and keep their shape. If you want to win prizes, your jelly should not be cloudy – so no squeezing the jelly bag!

PRESERVES usually refer to the whole fruit, sometimes cut into pieces, preserved in a syrup.

CONSERVES is honestly, I think, just a posh word for jam – and thus you can make expensive additions such as raisins, walnuts, chillies or citrus fruit.

MARMALADES are determined not by oranges, but by small slices of fruit (citrus, onion or rhubarb, for example) suspended in soft jelly.

FRUIT BUTTERS AND CHEESES are similar to jams but they are made with the fruit pulp, which is cooked with sugar until thick (here you can see the spoon's impression). A cheese is cooked with equal parts of sugar to fruit and is served sliced; a butter has half as much sugar, is softer in consistency and does not keep as long.

The four essential ingredients for all methods of jam-making are fruit, pectin, sugar and acid. While your choice of fruit clearly makes the jam, in terms of alchemy it is the pectin, sugar and acidity that make the gel.

On fruit

Your choice of fruit is up to you. Make sure it is ripe, but not overripe. If you want a good set, it's also a good idea to include a small percentage of underripe fruit because fruit loses pectin as it matures.

Pectin makes up part of the plant cell's wall; as fruit ripens the skin softens in part because the pectin begins to break down. This process can be exploited to make jam, since as you cook the fruit you release the pectin. In order to get the fruit to set again, you must offer up something for the pectin to bond to – this is the large dose of sugar, plus a rolling boil to evaporate some of the water. These things combined bring the pectin chains back together again, and miraculously your jam turns from syrup to jelly.

Some fruit contains more pectin than others (see page 132). One of the ways of boosting the pectin content of fruits that are low in pectin – berries, plums or cherries, for example – is to include a percentage of fruit that is rich in pectin, such as quinces, apples or citrus fruit. The alternative is to use jam sugar, commercial pectin or homemade pectin (see below). Commercial pectin is usually made from apples or the white pulp under the skin of citrus fruit.

HOMEMADE PECTIN It is very easy to make your own pectin and freeze it for later use – especially as commercial pectin is so expensive. I usually keep some in store for use with overripe berries.

I have given two recipes here for pectin, one using unripe apples and the other using crab apples, which are usually available from late September onwards. By using both, it should be possible to produce your own pectin all year round.

1) TART APPLE OR UNRIPE APPLE PECTIN

Remember you have to use unripe apples for this.

> 1.8kg whole unripe apples, cut into slices
> (including the cores)
> water

Place the sliced apples in a large pan with just enough water to allow them to float. Simmer for about 3–5 minutes or until the apples begin to soften. Once soft enough, press through a sieve or mouli to remove the cores.

Return the liquid and pulp to a jam pan (or similar heavy pan) and cook on a high heat until the mixture has reduced by half; avoid boiling at this stage.

Scoop the pulp into a clean pillowcase or muslin jelly bag and set aside to strain overnight. You can squeeze it if you are using this for jam, but if you want a clear jelly, then you're best leaving it alone.

Return the clear liquid to a clean pan and boil to reduce by just under half. Test for a set (see page 132) and reboil if necessary.

You can store your pectin in two ways. Either pour into bottles and waterbathe for 10 minutes at a rolling boil (see page 157), or place in an airtight container in the freezer. Pectin will keep for up to 12 months. Alternatively, you can use it straight away.

2) CRAB APPLE PECTIN

> 900g whole crab apples, sliced
> 750ml water

Place the crab apples in a large pan with the water. Simmer until the apples are tender, about 30 minutes, adding more water if necessary. Once soft, strain through a colander lined with muslin or a clean pillowcase into a clean bowl. Hopefully the juices will run clear; if they don't, reheat the liquid and strain again. Do not squeeze the muslin or you will end up with cloudy liquid.

Return the liquid to a clean pan and reduce by just under half. Test for a set (see page 132) and pour into bottles. Your pectin should taste much like unsweetened apple juice.

Testing your pectin levels (for homemade pectin)

It's a good idea to test how strong your homemade pectin is, otherwise you will end up having to guess how much to add to a recipe. You will need some methylated spirits to do this. Place 3 tablespoons methylated spirits in a glass jar and add 1 teaspoon of your cooled homemade pectin. Shake together and set aside for 1 minute. If the mixture coagulates into a jelly that you can pick up with a fork, you have successfully made a strong pectin. If not, return your liquid to the heat and boil a bit more. Do not taste the methylated spirit jelly – it is poisonous – and do not return it back to the pan to reboil!

How to test the pectin content of your fruit

Place a handful of your fruit in a bowl, pour over some boiling water and mash up to a purée. For harder fruits, simmer in a pan until soft. Place a tablespoon of the juice in a saucer and set aside to cool. Add 3 tablespoons methylated spirits to the cooled fruit juice, mix it in well and set aside to stand for 1 minute. If the mixture forms a single, large lump your fruit is rich in pectin; if you have 2 or 3 smaller lumps, your fruit should be ok and you can probably just get away with adding a little more lemon juice to get it to set. If you have lots of soft, little lumps, there is very little pectin in your fruit and you will need to either add commercial or homemade pectin to get it to set.

Natural pectin/acid levels of fruit

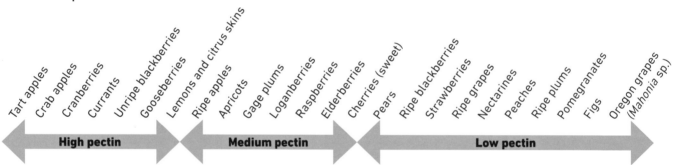

High pectin: Tart apples, Crab apples, Cranberries, Currants, Unripe blackberries, Gooseberries, Lemons and citrus skins

Medium pectin: Ripe apples, Apricots, Gage plums, Loganberries, Raspberries, Elderberries, Cherries (sweet)

Low pectin: Pears, Ripe blackberries, Strawberries, Ripe grapes, Nectarines, Peaches, Ripe plums, Pomegranates, Figs, Oregon grapes (Mahonia sp.)

How much homemade pectin do you add?

Well that's a bit of a difficult question to answer precisely, because this will be determined by the ripeness and natural pectins level of the fruit you are using to make your jam.

I tend to add homemade pectin to low-pectin jams like strawberry, pear, grape or cherry or blackberry. As a general rule of thumb, I allow approx. 60–110g pectin to every 450g fruit, adding it at the beginning with the raw fruit instead of water. Note that it is perfectly ok to boil homemade pectin, not like the commercial stuff (which you add towards the end of the jam-making process). Saying that, it is possible to add your homemade pectin towards the end and still get a good set, although I tend to add an extra tablespoon of lemon juice just to be on the safe side.

If your jam or jelly fails to set, this is usually a sign that it doesn't have enough good-quality pectin. The remedy here would be to add more pectin (at the end in the form of lemon juice) and quickly reboil.

On acid

Acid is a key component of gelling. Fruits that have a high pectin content tend to have high acidity. Underripe fruit tends to be more acidic than ripe fruit (no kidding, Sherlock).

In order for pectin to gel, acidity needs to be somewhere between 2.8 and 3.5pH – in taste terms, that's roughly the same as ripe lemon juice mixed with a little sugar. If your fruit is not as tart as this, you will need to add extra acid. As a guideline, allow approx. ½ teaspoon of citric acid or 2 tablespoons of lemon juice for every 1.8kg (4lb) of fruit.

On sugar

The basic rule for jam-making is equal parts sugar to fruit. In simple terms, to work out how much sugar you will need, just chop up your fruit, weigh it and add the same amount of sugar. However, that's a lot of sugar when you consider how much natural sugar your fruit already contains. If you want to cut down on the sugar, that is fine – just make sure it doesn't fall below the 60 per cent mark. So for 1kg fruit you should add 750g sugar. Note that low-sugar jam will not keep as well as high-sugar jam unless it is waterbathed (see page 157). Unless the pectin content of the fruit is high, these jams may set rather soft. Saying that, this ratio is perfect for small batches of jam (a jar or two) that you will eat up quickly

Equipment for jam and jelly-making

JAM PAN: this is indispensable because it has a thick bottom, which stops scorching and burning. Good versions have a measure up the side to allow you to accurately reduce the jam.

WOODEN SPOON (not one that it used for cooking onion or garlic)

JAM FUNNEL

MUSLIN STRAINING BAG (or a clean, ironed pillowcase – the ironing helps to sterilise it)

JAM LABELS

JAM JARS, WAX DISCS AND LIDS

SAUCERS: these should be kept in the fridge to test for setting point

SLOTTED SPOON: to remove any errant stones or scum (always do this at the end as your jam cools or you'll waste jam)

Top tips for successful jam-making

Choose ripe fruit, but also include a small percentage of underripe fruit (this will contain higher levels of pectin). Remember that overripe fruit makes for runny jam.

If you know that your fruit is low in pectin, either combine it with something rich in pectin – such as crab apples or redcurrants – or add homemade pectin or lemon juice. Alternatively, take a shortcut and use jam sugar (but this will hike up the cost of your jam).

If you follow either the commercial pectin or jam sugar route, stick to the manufacturer's instructions; they all vary a bit, but it is not for you to question why, just to follow. If this riles you, make your own pectin (see page 130).

If you don't know the pectin content of your fruit, test it (see page 132).

Never use iron pans; they react with the acid in the fruit. Invest in a jam pan!

HOW TO MAKE JAM

1) COOK YOUR FRUIT. Simmer the fruit until it is tender – this can take anything from 5 to 45 minutes. Remember 'slow and low' to break down the pectin chains; never boil at this stage.

2) ADD THE SUGAR. Allow 60–65 per cent sugar to 40 per cent fruit; any lower and the jam will ferment (which is shorthand for compost). If your sugar content is too high, your jam will crystallise. If you wish, you can preheat the sugar in the oven first on a very low heat. This helps it to dissolve faster into the jam and improves the colour.

3) BOIL UNTIL SETTING POINT IS REACHED. Once your sugar has dissolved, bring the jam to the boil (preferably without stirring too much). Boil hard to reach setting point. This can take up to 20 minutes (any longer and you destroy the reformed pectin chains).

To test for a set, either use the saucer or flake method (see page 140).

If you are using the saucer method, remember to turn off the jam while you wait for it to cool down on the saucer; failure to do this could result in overboiling your jam and ending up with something very hard!

4) SKIM AND START BOTTLING. Remove from the heat, skim off any scum (this is your reward, have bread and butter ready), give it a steady stir to distribute the fruit pieces evenly throughout the jam and start bottling. A jam funnel makes all the difference here. Fill your warm, sterilised jars almost to the top, leaving 1–2cm headroom. NB: jam shrinks as it ages so don't waste space. A jar that is not fully filled will go off more quickly because the increased space offers more opportunity for spoilage.

6) SEAL, LABEL AND STORE. Add a wax disc (the wax side goes down). If you do get mould, it will sit on top of the disc and not the jam. Cover with a lid, label and store in a cool, dark place.

Remember: the preserver here is sugar. If you haven't followed a recipe, or used the correct ratio of sugar to fruit (i.e. you forgot to weigh your ingredients), store your jam in the fridge and eat it up quickly.

Jellies need clarity. These are the stained-glass windows of the preserve world. Thus, they are strained (but not squeezed) to create a clear colour. You can use a jelly bag, pillowcase or large piece of muslin tied together to create a bag. If you do not have a purpose built jelly stand (and I don't, so no need to run out and get one) you will have to improvise. I use a bamboo cane balanced between a chair and the sideboard and hand the bag from that. You must boil your muslin or jelly bag between strainings to sterilise it. A hot iron is a good, quick way of sterilising it.

HOW TO MAKE JELLY

1) COOK YOUR FRUIT INTO A PULP. This can take up to an hour depending on the fruit. It should be simmered not boiled. You will need to add water to your fruit, but not so much it dilutes the flavour.

2) STRAIN YOUR FRUIT. Pour the pulp and juices very carefully into your jelly bag and strain. The pulp will be hot and could easily splatter, so it might be easiest to transfer it to a jug first rather than pouring directly from the pan. Never, ever squeeze the bag or you will end up with cloudy jelly. It normally takes between 1 and 10 hours for the juice to drip through; I usually strain overnight. (If you wish, you can use the pulp left in the bag to make cheese, butter or fruit leathers – see page 66 – but strain it first to remove the seeds.)

3) BOIL THE JUICE AND SWEETEN. Don't start this next stage unless you have at least an hour set aside to do so (I say this from miserable experience).

Pour the strained juice into a clean pan, bring to the boil and add the sugar – note that the sugar should not be added until it comes to the boil. If the strained juice seems too thin, you can always reduce it first before adding the sugar.

The amount of sugar added will depend on the pectin levels of your fruit (see page 132). If your fruit is low in pectin, use 1kg sugar per litre of juice. If the pectin level is high, use 600g sugar per litre of juice.

4) BOIL UNTIL SETTING POINT IS REACHED. Boil the jelly for 10 minutes or so without stirring before checking for a set. (Note that the longer you heat the juice and sugar together the darker the colour of the jelly.)

5) SKIM AND BOTTLE. Once setting point is reached, take the jelly off the heat and quickly remove any scum. Pour immediately into clean, warm, sterilised jars. (If you allow the jelly to sit in the pan too long it will start to set and this ruins the consistency, so time is of the essence here.) Ideally, the jars should be tilted and the jelly poured down the side so that you don't trap any bubbles. Carefully place on wax discs and seal the jars.

Do not disturb the jars until the jelly has set because this can cause air to get trapped inside, which affects storage.

If you have made jelly, you might as well make a cheese or butter with the leftover pulp. I think all fruit cheeses taste better after a week or so of sitting. However, butters don't keep for long – so use them up quickly. Fruit butters work well as a sweetener in homemade muesli. You can include spices and juice or cider instead of water if you wish to create various flavours.

HOW TO MAKE CHEESE (FROM WHOLE FRUIT)

1) COOK THE FRUIT. Cut the fruit into small pieces, place in a pan and cover with half the quantity of either water, fruit juice or cider. Bring to a simmer and cook until the fruit is soft.

2) STRAIN. Push your cooked fruit through a sieve or mouli. If necessary, purée with a masher, food-processor or hand-held blender. (If using strained leftover pulp from jelly-making, you should strain out the skin, seeds or stems using a mouli or colander before going on to the next step.)

3) ADD SUGAR. Place your purée (or pulp) in a pan. If it looks thin, simmer over a low heat until it thickens. Add 1kg sugar for every 1kg of pulp. If you wish, you could use less sugar than this (750g to 1kg), but you will have to cook it for much longer to reach setting point and it won't store as well.

4) COOK UNTIL THICK. Boil gently for about an hour until the mixture is stiff. You will need to stir it frequently to stop the mixture from burning. The cheese is ready when you can draw a spoon across the bottom of the pan and it leaves a clean line.

5) BOTTLE AND SEAL. Cheese is traditionally served whole, sliced – in which case you might want to pour it into a container or mould that can be turned out. Tea cups, wide-necked jars and other small containers are all suitable; you can seal the surface with hot food-grade wax (see suppliers) poured on top. Saying that, I tend to be lazy and just bottle it up as for jams in jars with lids.

HOW TO MAKE FRUIT BUTTER

1) COOK THE FRUIT PULP WITH SUGAR. The ideal thing to use for this is the leftover strained pulp from making jelly. Weigh the pulp and measure out half the quantity of sugar – so for 500g pulp you will need 250g sugar.

Place the pulp, sugar and any flavourings or spices in a large pan and heat until the sugar has dissolved. Bring to the boil and cook until the butter is thick and creamy with no excess liquid.

2) BOTTLE AND SEAL. Pour into clean, hot jars and seal. If you are planning to store your butter long-term, rather than use it up fairly quickly, it's best to waterbathe. If so, leave a gap of 5cm between the butter and lid when filling and process at a rolling boil for 15 minutes.

If you are going to use the jam up fairly quickly, fill to within 1cm of the lid, screw on the lid and invert the jar so it sits upside down for 5 minutes; then turn it the right way up and allow to cool naturally. The theory here is that because the butter is piping hot it will destroy any spoilage organisms and sterilise the area under the lid by creating a vacuum. However, there is a lot of controversy around this method. Many people think that the vacuum is not strong enough and any air left in the jar will invite mould. I think it's a good method for making sure the butter stores longer than a couple of weeks, but I wouldn't want to say that this method is failsafe.

Sterilising your jars

Perhaps the easiest way to sterilise jars is to run clean jars through the dishwasher without using detergent. However, if you neither own a dishwasher nor have enough jars to make this efficient you will need to wash your jars in soapy water, rinse them and then boil them in a large pan at 160°C for 10 minutes. Alternatively, preheat your oven to 180°C/gas mark 4 (no higher), place the jars on a baking sheet or rack lined with a thick layer of newspaper (making sure they are not touching) and heat for 20 minutes. Once sterilised, I tend to keep the jars in the oven until needed, so they remain warm. I always sterilise more jars than I need, in case of spillages, etc.

Never sterilise the lids in the oven – the temperature will ruin the rubber inside the rim; these should be boiled instead.

FILLING YOUR JARS Never add cold food to hot jars or hot food to cold jars. Spoon the mixture into the jars while the contents are still hot, place on wax discs and put the lids on and allow the contents to settle. After 15 minutes you can screw the lids on tightly; allow the jam to cool completely before storing in a cool, dark place.

QUANTITY OF JARS As you will see, some of the recipes don't state how many jars you will need. This says a lot about me and my love of oddly shaped jam jars. It also says a lot about jam making. The age of your fruit, how much liquid you add, how long you cook for will effect the amount of preserve made. But if you like precision then here is roughly how it works: to determine the weight the quantity of sugar should be multiplied by 10 and divided by 6 (the assumption here is that you are using the same weight of fruit as sugar).

Setting point

Setting point is the magical moment when the jam sets so that it is no longer runny. Unfortunately most of the time you can't see this happen – there are hints, but as it doesn't set in the pan you'll need to do a test to check.

FLAKE TEST The flake test is considered to be one of the best tests, although it does take a bit of practice. Dip a wooden spoon into the jam, remove it and turn it on its side. Allow the jam to cool slightly and watch as it runs off the spoon. If the jam collects and hangs there, eventually dropping off in a clear manner, the jam is done. Turn off the heat immediately. This will make a very firm jam (or a perfect jelly). For a softer set the jam should hang on the edge of spoon briefly and then roll off. After a bit of practice, you should be able to tell immediately what stage you are at. In the meantime, use the plate test to help you out.

PLATE TEST This the easiest method for a beginner, but it takes time – so if you do not turn the heat off between tests you run the risk of overboiling your jam. Place three or four saucers/small plates in the fridge (or freezer if you have room) to cool. When you think your jam might be ready, take ½ teaspoon or so of jam and place it on the cold plate. Allow it to cool slightly. If you can make the jam wrinkle by pushing it with your finger, it is fully set, if you can run your finger through the jam to separate it, it is minutes away from being set. Use too much jam or a warm plate and valuable time is lost.

TEMPERATURE TEST If all else fails, you can use a jam thermometer – just make sure it is a proper jam or sweet thermometer that can reach the high temperatures. Make sure you stir your jam before taking the temperature. When the temperature reaches 110°C the jam is set.

GOOSEBERRY AND ELDERFLOWER JAM

Inspired by Particular Delights *by Nathalie Hambro*

- 800g granulated sugar
- 1kg gooseberries
- 500ml water
- 5 elderflower heads in a muslin bag.
  *(if elderflowers are not in season, use
  4 tablespoons elderflower cordial
  concentrate)*
- sterilised jam jars with lids (see page
  138); *how many depends on the size of
  your jars, but makes roughly 1.4kg*

Preheat the oven to 100°C. Warm the sugar in an ovenproof dish until it is just hot to the touch and glistening. (Heating the sugar helps it to dissolve more quickly when added to the pan, meaning you don't end up overcooking the gooseberries and they keep their shape.)

Meanwhile, top and tail the gooseberries. Place them in a preserving pan with the water and elderflowers (or elderflower cordial) and heat slowly until the gooseberries start to soften. Put in the hot sugar and stir once to dissolve. Do not stir continuously or the gooseberries will break up. Bring to a gentle boil for 20–30 minutes until setting point is reached (test for this using the plate method, see page 140).

Once set, allow the jam to cool slightly before skimming off any scum (there may be quite a bit). Ladle into warm, sterilised jars, cover with wax discs and seal. As Nathalie Hambro suggests, this jam is made for buttery croissants.

RHUBARB AND GINGER JAM

This recipe is a favourite in many old jam books. I adapted it slightly by adding some cinnamon and a little orange juice.

- 2kg rhubarb, cut into 2cm chunks
- 1.75kg–2kg light brown sugar
- 100g chopped crystallised ginger *(grated fresh ginger could be used instead but you might need to add more sugar)*
- 225ml orange juice
- 1 small cinnamon stick
- juice of 2 lemons (or 1 level teaspoon citric acid)
- sterilised jam jars with lids (see page 138); *how many depends on the size of your jars*

Wash and dry the rhubarb, layer it up with the sugar in a large non-reactive bowl, cover with a tea-towel and set aside to macerate somewhere cool overnight. The following morning, most of the sugar will be dissolved and the rhubarb will be sitting in its own juices.

Tip the contents of the bowl into a preserving pan, add the ginger, orange juice, cinnamon stick and lemon juice (or citric acid) and slowly bring to the boil, stirring. Boil rapidly until the rhubarb is tender and the jam reaches setting point, about 30 minutes (see page 140). Pour into warm, sterilised jars and seal.

RHUBARB AND ELDERFLOWER JAM

This jam locks in the flavours of June. I think it works best if the recipe is not rushed – that 24-hour soak is everything to the subtleness of the elderflower.

- 450g rhubarb, cut into 2cm chunks
- 5 large elderflower heads
- 450g golden granulated sugar *(preferably sugar that has had a vanilla bean pod scenting it)*
- juice of 1 lemon
- sterilised jars with lids (see page 138); *how many depends on the size of your jars*

Wash and dry the rhubarb then place it in a large non-reactive bowl with the elderflowers and sugar. Cover with a tea-towel and set aside in warm place for 24 hours to draw out the juices. The following day, the rhubarb should be swimming in syrup.

Tip the contents of your bowl into a preserving pan, add the lemon juice and heat gently to dissolve the sugar. Simmer over a low heat until the rhubarb is soft and pulpy, but not entirely disintegrated, about 30 minutes. Once the rhubarb has softened, bring to the boil and boil rapidly until set, about 10 minutes. I like this set soft, rather than firm. It suits the gentle nature of the flavours and makes it all the better when dolloped in yogurt. Pour into warm, sterilised jars and seal.

STRAWBERRY CONSERVE

Either you see this jam as taking an extraordinarily long time, or you see it as adaptable to your busy schedule. Well timed and you can do all the cooking before breakfast. The point of this jam is that the strawberries are left whole and the long soak allows them to squish into something heavenly. This jam is not for long storage.

If this is all too much, hull and chop strawberries, add lemon juice and sugar and cook as you would any other jam – in which case it will store for longer than a conserve.

> 1kg strawberries *(pick the smaller varieties for conserve and use large ones for making jam)*
> 1kg golden granulated sugar
> juice of 1 lemon
> sterilised jam jars with lids (see page 138); *how many depends on the size of your jars*

Layer up the strawberries in a large, wide pan with the sugar and set aside to macerate for 24 hours.

The following day, the strawberries will be sitting in their own juice. Tip into a preserving pan and bring to the boil and boil gently for no more than 5 minutes. Cover with a tea-towel and set aside for a further 24 hours (you can set it aside for up to 3 days if necessary).

The following day, add the lemon juice and slowly bring the strawberries back to the boil and boil rapidly until set (see page 140), about 20 minutes.

To stop the strawberries floating to the top of the pot, allow the jam to cool slightly so that a skin forms on the surface before bottling. Pour slowly into warm, sterilised jars and seal.

ADDING DIFFERENT FLAVOURS This method works if you want to make a lot of small batches of jam with varying flavours (say strawberry jam flavoured with geranium, mint or black pepper). It is especially useful when deciding which route to take, or if you don't want jars and jars of a particular flavour – black pepper and strawberry jam is great with goat's cheese, but you don't need a whole larder full of the stuff.

Preheat your oven to 140°C/gas mark 2 and warm the sugar for 15 minutes – just so it is hot to the touch. Meanwhile, prepare your fruit and put it in a jam pan. Pour the hot sugar over the fruit and bring to a gentle simmer, stirring to dissolve the sugar. Once the sugar has dissolved, switch off the heat and leave to macerate overnight in the oven. In the morning you can remove small batches (a couple of jars' worth) at a time, add your flavours and bring back to the boil until setting point is reached.

WILD STRAWBERRY JAM

This is a heavenly jam, but it is almost impossible to collect 500g wild strawberries at once (unless you have happened upon a forest of them). Instead, pick and freeze them in batches until you have enough. It is a delicious jam to enjoy at the end of summer, but not worth storing away (it's too runny and will only get runnier with time).

> 500g wild strawberries
> 750g caster sugar
> juice of ½ lemon
> sterilised jam jars with lids (see page 138); *how many depends on the size of your jars*

Place the strawberries in a bowl, add the sugar and stir very gently to combine. Set aside somewhere warm for several hours until the juices run pink.

Tip into a preserving pan, add the lemon juice, bring slowly to the boil to dissolve the sugar and boil rapidly for 10 minutes (not too long or the strawberries will disintegrate). Pour into warm, sterilised jars and seal. This jam will not set well. Run with its sloppiness and spoon it into Greek yogurt or let it race across butter.

ROASTED PLUM, CARDAMOM AND VANILLA JAM

2kg plums
a generous handful of soft dark
   brown sugar
2kg light brown sugar
1 split vanilla pod
1 teaspoon cardamom seeds, finely
   ground (optional)
juice of 2 lemons
sterilised jam jars with lids (see page
   138); *how many depends on the size*
   of your jars

Preheat your oven to 140°C/gas mark 2. Cut the plums in half and destone them. Place skin-side down in a large roasting tin and sprinkle over the dark brown sugar. Roast in the oven for 40 minutes, checking them regularly to make sure they don't burn.

Layer up the cooked plums in a large bowl with the light brown sugar and bury the vanilla pod in among them. Set aside for at least 3 hours to macerate, preferably overnight. (If you are pushed for time you can omit this stage, but I do think it makes the jam. The plums truly begin to soften so you end up with wonderful whole mouthfuls of plums rather than just a sticky mass.)

Tip the contents of the bowl into a preserving pan and add the cardamom (if using) and lemon juice. Bring slowly to the boil, stirring to dissolve the sugar, and then boil rapidly for 20 minutes until thick and setting point is reached (see page 140). Let the jam cool slightly and skim off any scum. Pour (or ladle) into warm, sterilised jars and seal.

DAMSON CHEESE

Damson cheese is best potted into jars that are small with a wide neck. This way, you can decant the entire cheese to be served up with cheese, meats or just as an indulgent pudding with a great dollop of thick cream and a little port poured over. The cheese should be a deep, dark velvety purple. The best way to achieve this is to pick from a gnarled old tree – those smaller, uncultivated damsons make for the best preserve.

1kg damsons
100ml water
approx. 1kg granulated sugar
sterilised jars with lids (see page 138);
   how many depends on the size of
   your jars

Preheat the oven to 140°C/gas mark 2. Place the damsons and water in a large roasting tin and cook in the oven until the juices run freely and the stones are loose, about 30 minutes. Allow to cool slightly, and then strain through a nylon sieve, pressing the pulp through with a wooden spoon. Crack a few of the stones, remove the kernels and add them to the pulp (these impart a lovely almondy flavour).

To calculate how much sugar you will need, weigh out your pulp and weigh out the same quantity of sugar. If your preserving pan has a measure down the side, for every pint of pulp add a pound of sugar. Otherwise, if you have 1.5kg of pulp you will need just under 1.5kg of sugar. While the oven is still hot, place the sugar in an ovenproof bowl and heat until it is just hot to the touch and starting to glisten.

Place the damson pulp and the hot sugar in a preserving pan and heat gently, stirring constantly to dissolve the sugar. Simmer until the cheese thickens: it is ready when you can draw a spoon across the base of the pan and it leaves a clean line. Pour into warm, sterilised wide-mouthed jars and use a clean skewer (or chopstick) to dislodge any air bubbles. Seal, label and store as for jam.

RASPBERRY JAM

I like an unadulterated jam and this is the simplest method I've found. This recipe is perfectly adaptable for any quantity – whether you have a bowlful of raspberries or a basketload.

raspberries
sugar
sterilised jam jars with lids (see page 138);
   how many depends on the size of your
   jars

Weigh your raspberries and put them in a dish with the same quantity of sugar. Set aside somewhere warm until the juices run.

Bring the raspberries slowly to the boil in a preserving pan, stirring to dissolve the sugar, and boil rapidly until setting point is reached, about 5 minutes. Pot while still hot into warm, sterilised jars, label and store.

NO-SUGAR RASPBERRY JAM

If you don't want to rely so much on refined sugar, you could substitute honey or fruit juice concentrate (apple juice concentrate is my favourite). Once jam is liberated from sugar, the flavour becomes quite something – although the drawback is it will often be much runnier, more like a fruit spread or compote unless you add gelatine or agar agar flakes. Agar agar flakes can be found in health found shops and Asian markets. Their jelly-like properties are very strong and require very little heat to be effective, so don't overboil. Agar agar doesn't make soft set jam, it really makes it more like a jelly.

These low-sugar jams won't store for such long periods (unless stored in the freezer). Jams made in this way must be stored in the fridge once opened, especially if you're using fruit juice concentrate. However, I defy anyone to keep this jam for long.

This recipe for raspberry jam will store for 3–4 weeks in the fridge, unopened, so only make a small batch.

raspberries
apple juice concentrate
lemon juice
agar agar flakes (follow manufacturer's
   instructions, roughly a teaspoon for
   every 250ml liquid)
sterilised jam jars with lids (see page 138);
   how many depends on the size of your
   jars

Gently wash the raspberries under running water and place in a heavy-based pan. Add the apple juice concentrate – this should be done to taste, but you want roughly a third of the volume in apple juice concentrate. Bring the mixture to the boil for around 5 minutes. At this point lemon juice can be added if wanted. Stirring continuously, continue to boil for another 5 minutes and add the agar agar flakes. Boil for another minute or so. You should start to see the mixture gel considerably. Take off the heat and bottle the jam in clean, sterilised jars. This jam must be kept in the fridge. However, it is possible to store it in the freezer. If you want to do this make sure you leave expansion room in the jar (fill up to ¾ full).

REDCURRANT JELLY

A similar jelly can be made with rowanberries.

> 900g redcurrants
> 300ml water
> granulated sugar
> sterilised jam jars with lids (see page
> 138); *how many depends on the size of
> your jars*

Strip the fruit from the stalks and wash. Place the fruit in a pan with the water and simmer gently until the redcurrants are quite soft. Crush well with a potato masher or the back of a spoon.

Pour into a jelly bag or clean, ironed pillowcase and strain overnight. (If you're in a hurry and don't care about having a completely clear jelly, you can squeeze out as much pulp as possible – just don't think of entering the local horticultural show as this is going to be a cloudy-looking jelly!)

Measure the juice and for every pint (568ml) of juice add a pound (450g) of sugar (you can use slightly less, say 12oz (340g), but this will not store for long or it will need waterbathing (process for 5 minutes on a rolling boil in a waterbath).

Place the juice in the preserving pan and bring to the boil, add the sugar and stir until fully dissolved. Boil rapidly until the jelly sets. Skim quickly and pot in warm sterilised jars, covering the jelly with a wax disc and a lid.

Don't waste the pulp!

Don't waste the redcurrant pulp; it can be made into excellent fruit leather (see page 66). Strain it through a mouli to get rid of the pips and skins*, add a suitable amount of sugar (55g for every 200g fruit), or honey to taste, and spread over baking paper. Transfer to a dehydrator or low oven at 70°C until dry to the touch.

* If you wish, the pips and skins can be used to flavour cider vinegar. Pop them into a bottle of vinegar and set aside in a dark, cool place to infuse for a week or so. This vinegar is particularly good for using in pickles.

MARROW AND GINGER JAM

There is always a moment when those baby courgettes turn into marrows overnight. You can use marrows to bulk up chutney or relishes, brew strange rum or make into jam. I dislike the overly sweet nature of most marrow jams, but this one is quite divine. It's an old favourite for a reason. You can add cinnamon or cardamom for something a little more exotic – just add a small quill or a few bruised cardamom pods to the muslin bag. This jam improves greatly with age and tends to darken in colour. Wait at least 3 months before opening.

> 1 large marrow, roughly 2kg, or several
>   smaller ones to the same weight
> 2kg granulated sugar
> 4 unwaxed lemons
> 1 x 5cm piece of fresh root ginger, peeled
>   and sliced
> sterilised jam jars with lids (see page
>   138), *how many depends on the size of
>   your jars*

Peel the marrow and cut into 2cm cubes, discarding any seeds or woody bits. In a large pan, layer the marrow with the sugar; cover with a tea-towel and set aside to macerate for up to 24 hours, tossing occasionally. This process draws out the moisture from the marrows and helps them to hold their shape in the jam.

Juice the lemons and set aside. Place the halved lemon skins, any pips and the ginger into a muslin bag and tie. Tip the marrow, along with all the syrup, into a preserving pan and add the muslin bag and lemon juice. Bring slowly to the boil, stirring to dissolve the sugar, and then simmer for about 30 minutes until the marrow is translucent and the jam has set. If you cook the jam too vigorously then you will destroy the shape of the marrow. You don't want a firm set for this one, so don't overboil. Remove the muslin bag and allow the jam to cool a little so that a skin forms on top. Remove any scum and ladle into warm, sterilised jars, cover and label.

ON BOTTLING

There is a moment when jam is not enough, when pickles will not suffice and, frankly, the thought of having to rehydrate tomatoes is just a step too far for supper. This is where bottling boldly steps in. All you need is a bubbling vat of hot water, jars filled with your precious harvest, a timer and a little patience and you have contents that will survive a year or more on your shelves. As someone who has neither the space nor the inclination to own a chest freezer, bottling is my route to large-scale storage of summer crops. There are many options, from bottled fruits for pies to whole tomatoes, passata, sauces, salsas and low- or no-sugar fruit spreads or butters.

Once you've bottled the first batch, and there they sit cooling on the sideboard, a wave of happiness floods over you. If you thought jam made you happy, wait until you bottle. It is a near-religious experience, a step closer to self-reliance, another month off from the tyranny of supermarket shopping and, much more importantly, a route to great meals.

Preparation is everything to bottling. Once the jars are submerged in the boiling water, there is little to do but wait until their time is up and not jostle them around too much. It is quite true that for those with huge harvests and acres of land, bottling is a task that will take up days and require many hands to keep those pots bubbling and the next round prepared. But it is quite possible to do it on a much smaller scale, to preserve a few jars at a time as your harvest ripens, and this will take a matter of hours at the most.

HOW BOTTLING WORKS

There are two ways of bottling: either in a waterbath or in a pressure cooker. The waterbath is used for high-acid foods; the pressure cooker is used for more complicated contents such as seafood, meat and low-acid foods. There are no recipes in this book where you'd have to use a pressure cooker.

Bottling preserves the contents by applying heat and excluding air to create a vacuum. The heat destroys potential spoilage organisms that might make the food inedible or even dangerous, it also drives out air creating a vacuum. The seal protects the contents from outside contamination during storage – that is until you open the jar, and break the seal, and then the contents should be stored in the fridge and used up immediately.

Depending on the acidity of the food, the jars are submerged in a waterbath on a rolling boil for a period of time, anything from 10 to 80 minutes. This rolling boil penetrates the contents of the jar from the outside. What is essential is that all the contents are heated up. The size of the jar will affect the boiling time, with bigger or wider jars taking longer; for this reason it is never wise to bottle a variety of different-shaped jars at the same time.

Waterbathing is ideal for strong acid foods – that is anything lower than 4.6pH – mainly fruits, including tomatoes, pickles, relishes and cooked sweet spreads, butters (see page 138) and low- or no-sugar jams. If the contents are not naturally lower than 4.6 pH, you need to add acid usually in the form of lemon juice or citric acid.

Some older books and texts recommend pasteurising your filled bottles in the oven as opposed to a waterbath. However, this method is no longer considered acceptable (although sterilising *empty* jars in the oven is fine) because dry heat does not penetrate the jars as well as wet heat (and there's also the minor factor of the glass jars exploding). Some texts also recommend inverting the filled jars instead of waterbathing, the idea being that the hot liquid will expel any air and sterilise the contents. This does not work either.

HYGIENE Hygiene is key with this method of preservation. No matter how hot your waterbath gets, it still makes sense to limit the number of organisms that could get inside your jars in the first place. Make sure everything is scrupulously clean – wash you hands, your utensils, sterilise your jars, lids and screw bands and ensure that you process properly – then there is little danger.

Waterbathing equipment

In the States, picking up a waterbath or canner is simple; any DIY store carries the famous blue enamel pots and racks. You could try importing one, but I've found the delivery costs can be prohibitively expensive. Of course, you could scour car boot sales for old models. The European version tends to be oval and made out of aluminium; a grandparent might still have one. Alternatively, with a little ingenuity you could adapt a saucepan to create a perfectly good product of your own.

I take waterbathing seriously and actually own two waterbaths, a large industrial pot with an American rack (that allows me to lift out all the jars in one go) and a homemade version designed for processing smaller quantities. I brought the rack back in my suitcase from the States and then went to a commercial cooking equipment shop to buy the pot. Not exactly the cheapest method, but it does allow me to process a large number of jars at once – say for tomatoes or salsas.

Mostly, however, I just want to bottle very small batches – perhaps two or three jars at the most. My tomato harvests are sporadic (thanks to our wet summers) and if I'm gifted a bag of plums or pick up some windfall apples it simply doesn't make sense to heat up that great huge pan for such a small batch. So I improvised. I bought a very cheap, thin, large stock pan from my local ethnic food market, and then I added a steaming rack as a false bottom (a cake rack works just as well or several screw bands from Mason-style glass jars that are no longer fit for use, tied together). The most important part is that the glass jars don't stand on the base of the pan on the direct heat (otherwise they'll explode) and the water can circulate freely around them. The pan needs to be deep enough that your jars are totally submerged in the water, including the lids, and there must be enough headroom for the water to boil hard without slopping over the top. This means a pan at least 45cm deep to hold 1 litre bottles. As a basic rule of thumb, allow for the depth of your jar plus 20cm headroom.

Jars

You cannot use recycled jam jars for waterbathing as these don't usually have thick enough glass to withstand being boiled. They will just end up popping and smashing. Also, you need a seal that is in perfect condition; a 'used' lid is never suitable.

There is a whole range of jars suitable for heat processing: Kilner and Mason jars have screw-top lids with a separate disc that you replace each time (cutting down costs); Weck or Le Parfait jars have a rubber-ring seal held in place by a glass lid that is clipped into place (these are preferable because there is no BPA plastic in the rings); and then there are the Bormioli Quattro Stagioni jars from Italy, with screw-on lids that need to be replaced each time. As none of these jars is cheap, you will start to feel decidedly stingy about giving away your bottled produce and letting your jars go, particularly if you know the user is liable to toss them in the recycling. A little education is required; I don't mind if I know they are being reused, but the idea of them ending up in the recycling bin breaks my heart.

Whichever style of jar you choose, make sure the disc or seal is in pristine condition and discard any that are degraded or flawed (as this will affect the vacuum). Old seals can be reused for dry storage; just mark them with an X so you don't get confused. You can get reconditioned Kilner and Le Parfait jars, but they are probably best saved for jam rather than bottling. I cannot stress enough that the contents will only remain vacuum-sealed if the jars are in prime condition.

Never put cold jars of food into very hot water (they may crack) and likewise don't fill the jar with boiling hot contents and then put it into a cold waterbath (cracking again). Always follow the procedure to heat the jars up first and then fill with the hot contents. It is very important to carefully follow the instructions of the manufacturer for waterbathing their jar (see sourcebook for websites). Each design has its nuances and if the instructions are not followed correctly the jar will not be safe for long storage.

Equipment for waterbathing

WATERBATH (see page 157)

JARS SUITABLE FOR HEAT PROCESSING: e.g. Kilner or Mason-style jars (see page 157)

WIDE-MOUTHED FUNNEL for filling jars

JAR LIFTERS e.g. rubber-covered tongs that allow you to lift the jars out of the boiling water (otherwise you have to leave the jars in the water until the water cools down; this will slow you down if you're making several batches)

CLEAN TEA-TOWELS

DAMP, CLEAN CLOTH for wiping around the lid of the jars

MEASURING SPOONS

HOW TO BOTTLE

1) WASH AND STERILISE YOUR JARS. One of the simplest methods is to wash your jars in the dishwasher. Alternatively, wash by hand, air dry and sterilise in the oven at 180°C/gas mark 4 for 20 minutes. Remove with thick oven mitts and stand on an ovenproof mat, wooden chopping board or doubled up tea-towel. Never place lids or seals in the dishwasher or they will degrade. Pop them into a clean saucepan and pour over boiling water to sterilise instead.

2) PREPARE THE INGREDIENTS. All the recipes in this book are hot-packed, which means the contents are hot when they go into the jars. This is considered to be one of the safest methods. It also reduces the length of time needed in the waterbath (and when that kettle gets steaming you will be grateful for that).

3) FIRE UP YOUR WATERBATH. Although it would seem simple enough to line up your jars in a row and fill them up, this would mean exposing them to open-air spoilers while they are standing waiting to be filled. Instead, it is better to keep them waiting in the waterbath while you finish off preparing the contents.

Fill your warm sterilised jars with hot water from the tap, place the filled jars in the waterbath and bring the pan of water to the boil. Boil rapidly for 10 minutes on a rolling boil. Place the lids and bands/seals in a separate saucepan. When your ingredients are ready for bottling, only remove one of the jars at a time. Carefully empty out the hot water from inside the jar over the lids and bands to sterilise them. Fill the jar (see page 161) and put on the lids before going on to the next one.

4) FILL THE JARS. Here is the important bit. How full should your jar be? To start with, you cannot process a jar that is half full (so that's your supper sorted) – not only will your jar float in the waterbath (rather than staying submerged), but there will be far too much air inside the jar so the contents will spoil. Saying that, you don't want to overfill the jar either. If you top the jar up too much, the contents will end up oozing out into the waterbath as they bubble up inside like a mini volcano. That will not be fun to clean up and your jar will fail to form a perfect vacuum. So what you need to leave is some headroom. The amount of headroom varies according to the recipe, but it is usually 0.8–1.5cm. Remember steam in the headroom will expand more at higher altitudes than at sea level, so if you live on a mountain you will have to give a little more room. The maximum headroom you should allow is 4.5cm for a 1 litre bottle.

5) REMOVE AIR BUBBLES. The next step is to remove any large bubbles that may be trapped around the sides of the jar or among the contents. I find a sterilised chopstick is the best thing to use; do not use a knife or you could damage the glass jar. Just carefully poke the bubble so that the contents reshuffle. Be careful not to add more bubbles as you go. Generally, hot-packed contents have few bubbles, so you're just aiming to get rid of any large bubbles over 1mm.

6) SEAL YOUR JARS. Once the jar is full (with sufficient headroom), wipe down the mouth of the jar with a damp cloth. Fish out the flat disc from the hot water with tongs, place it centrally on the lid and add a screw band. (If working with Weck jars, place the rubber ring on the jar first, then put on the glass lid and finally attach the clips.) It's common sense really; the seal has to be on the lid, not partly on, or just off centre, but bang in the middle. If it's not fitted exactly, it won't seal. (A Weck jar is properly sealed if the lip on the rubber seal points downwards.) Tighten the lid to finger tightness – don't overscrew or you'll never get it off

again – place the jar in the waterbath and on to the next empty jar.

7) WATERBATHE YOUR JARS. Once all the jars are in the waterbath, bring it back to a rolling boil and start the timer. It must be a rolling boil when you start the timer. Don't worry that some of the jars have been sitting in the waterbath for some time already; it's the timing of the rolling boil that matters. The processing time will vary according to the recipe and depends both on the size of the jar and whether or not the contents are puréed or left whole. If you live at high altitude (i.e. over 3,000 feet), adjust the time as follows: for recipes that state 20 minutes at a rolling boil, increase the time by 1 minute for every 1,000 feet above sea level; for recipes that state more than 20 minutes, allow an additional 2 minutes per 1,000 feet above sea level.

8) REMOVE YOUR JARS. Once you have reached the allotted time, take the lid off the waterbath and wait 5 minutes for the contents to settle before removing the jars with tongs (if you don't have tongs, you can allow the waterbath to cool completely before removing the jars). This settling process ensures a good seal; if you take them out too soon some of the juice could spew out around the lids and destroy the seal. Place the jars very carefully on a folded tea-towel on your worksurface. Remember, you don't want to dislodge the contents.

9) CHECK THE SEALS. Allow the jars to cool for 1 hour and then carefully check the seals. If using Mason or Kilner jars, check that the safety seal has popped and is depressed (in the centre of the lid). For Weck jars, carefully remove the clips and check that you cannot lift off the glass lid.

Mark any jars that have not sealed properly with a cross. (These should be stored in the fridge and used up immediately.) The remaining jars should be left alone for 12–14 hours (essentially overnight) before labelling and storing. Store somewhere cool (10°C) out of direct sunlight.

APPLE SAUCE

Now I can see that it is quite easy to dismiss apple sauce, particularly an apple sauce with nothing but apples in it – no sugar, no spices, not a hint of anything other – but the best thing about this recipe is its adaptability. A sauce made from windfalls in autumn can be served with porridge in December, used in apple sauce cake (it can also be used as a substitute for butter if you add a little vegetable oil to it), used with pork and cabbage, thrown into winter squash or parsnip soup, added to meatballs as a binder, used in chutney, jams or fruit smoothies… the list goes on and on.

I think it's best to mix your apples, using some sweet dessert along with a cooker or two: I often use rosy red wild crab apples as well for colour. It doesn't matter much that they all have different cooking times because the sauce is puréed at the end. It is far quicker if you have a good mouli with fine holes, as this cuts out the peeling stage – all you need to do is core the apples first. However if you do not have one, no worries, just peel, core and dice the apples, cook until soft and blend in a food-processor (or mash with a potato masher for a chunkier sauce). NB: If you peel and core, you may find that you have less sauce than if you use a mouli.

> apples, *preferably a mixture of cooking and dessert apples* – **2.7kg will yield approx. 2.2 litres sauce**
> sugar or honey, to taste
> **mouli-style food mill**
> **500ml sterilised jars suitable for heat processing** *(e.g. Kilner jars, see page 157)*

Core your apples and cut into slices about 2.5cm thick. Place in a preserving pan and cover with 2cm water. Put on a lid, bring to the boil and simmer over a low heat for 30–50 minutes until the apples are tender, stirring occasionally. If necessary, you may need to add a little more water to stop the apples from sticking.

While your apple sauce is cooking, fill your waterbath. Fill the sterilised jars with warm water, put them in the waterbath and boil rapidly for 10 minutes on a rolling boil. Place the lids and bands/seals in a separate saucepan.

Transfer the apples to a food mill, mouli or food processor and process to a smooth purée. Taste and add a little sugar or honey if you wish. Depending on how much sugar you add, you may need to return the pan to the heat to dissolve the sugar.

Carefully lift the hot jars from the waterbath, empty out the water into the saucepan containing the lids and bands to sterilise them, and place the jars on a clean tea-towel. Fill the hot jars with apple sauce, leaving 1.5cm headroom (see page 161). Wipe the rims of the jars with a damp tea-towel, fish out the lids from the saucepan and fit them centrally on top. Put on the rings and tighten them so they are finger tight (no more or you'll never get them off again). Return the jars to the waterbath, making sure they are totally submerged, and process at a rolling boil for 20 minutes.

Take the lid off the waterbath, wait 5 minutes for the contents of the jars to settle, and then remove them very carefully with tongs. Set aside on a tea-towel for 1 hour before checking the seals (see page 161).

Avoid moving the jars for a further 12 hours (this is very important because you don't want to disturb the seals). Label and store in a cool, dark place (0–10 °C) and your purée should keep for up to a year.

NO-SUGAR FRUIT SPREAD

It is possible to make a whole fruit jam with no added sugar. It is hard to provide a precise recipe for such a jam, as so much depends on the fruit's water content and sugars.

I think the best way to make this is with very ripe fruit or fruits that are naturally very sweet. Grapes and plums are all ideal, perhaps with a few added redcurrants for tartness and much needed acidity. Apples, I think, just make for mush, so stay clear of these.

> sweet ripe fruit of your choice – *e.g.*
> *grapes, pears, plums*
> lemon juice *(necessary for pear as it is
> too low in acid).*
> 500ml sterilised jars suitable for heat
> processing *(e.g. Kilner jars, see page
> 157)*

Destone your fruit if necessary and cut into chunks. In a preserving pan, place a 2cm layer of fruit, crushed, to start the juices off and then add the rest of the fruit and bring to the boil. If there's not enough juice add just a little water, no more than 100ml for every 200g fruit. Simmer until the fruit is soft and then strain through a nylon sieve to remove the pips, skins or stalks. Return the strained fruit to the preserving pan and place the pips, etc. in a muslin bag – the pips, in particular, will hold some pectin necessary for the jam to set. Pop the muslin bag into the pan with the fruit. Cook over a very, very low heat until the jam is ready, stirring regularly as this jam often sticks to the pot. Add a tablespoon of fresh lemon juice for every 150g of pulp (roughly ¾ of pint of pulp). The jam is ready when it no longer drips off a wooden spoon but hangs (and eventually falls) off in a blob.

While your jam is cooking, fill your waterbath. Fill your sterilised jars with warm water, put them in the waterbath and boil rapidly for 10 minutes on a rolling boil. Place the lids and bands/seals in a separate saucepan. Carefully lift the hot jars from the waterbath, empty out the water into the saucepan containing the lids and bands to sterilise them, and place the jars on a clean tea-towel.

Fill the hot jars with jam, leaving 1cm headroom (see page 161). Wipe the rims of the jars with a damp tea-towel, fish out the lids from the saucepan and fit them centrally on top. Put on the rings and tighten them so they are finger tight (no more or you'll never get them off again). Return the jars to the waterbath, making sure they are totally submerged, and process at a rolling boil for 20 minutes.

Take the lid off the waterbath, wait 5 minutes to allow the contents of the jars to settle, and then remove the jars very carefully with tongs. Set aside on a tea-towel for 1 hour before checking the seals (see page 161).

Avoid moving the jars for a further 12 hours (this is very important because you don't want to disturb the seals). Label and store in a cool, dark place (0–10°C); this jam should keep for up to a year.

GRAPE JUICE CONCENTRATE

Every year I make a dark, intensely rich grape juice concentrate, which I then use as a sweetener in all manner of dishes including others jams (although it dyes everything its deep purple colour). Or it can be diluted into a fantastic juice. I grow the grape variety 'Brandt', which is hugely prolific and always gives me many bunches of small, heavily pipped grapes. These are perfect for grape concentrate.

    grapes
    boiling water
    500ml or 1 litre jars suitable for heat
        processing *(e.g. Mason jars, see page 157) – I litre bottles are more suitable if you are making juice*

Wash your grapes and place them in a preserving pan with enough boiling water to cover. Simmer for about 30 minutes until the skins soften and burst, and then strain through a double layer of muslin or jelly bag. At this point, the juice will contain a lot of sediment, so set it aside for 24 hours to allow the sediment to drop to the bottom.

The following day, carefully pour off the clear juice into a clean preserving pan, leaving the sediment behind. I like to reduce the grape juice so that it is slightly viscous, thus evaporating a little more water and sweetening it ever so. If you wish, you could add sugar to taste at this point, but I think the joy here is the natural flavour.

Meanwhile, fill your waterbath. Fill your sterilised jars with warm water, put them in the waterbath and boil rapidly for 10 minutes on a rolling boil. Place the lids and bands/seals in a separate saucepan. Carefully lift the hot jars from the waterbath, empty out the water into the saucepan containing the lids and bands to sterilise them, and place the jars on a clean tea-towel. Your grape concentrate should go into your jars hot, so if necessary transfer to a pot and bring quickly and briefly to the boil.

Fill the hot jars with the grape concentrate, leaving 1cm headroom (see page 161). Wipe the rims of the jars with a damp tea-towel, fish out the flat lids/bands from the saucepan and fit them centrally on top. Put on the rings/clips and tighten them so they are finger tight (no more or you'll never get them off again). Return the jars to the waterbath, making sure they are totally submerged, and process at a rolling boil for 15 minutes.

Take the lid off the waterbath, wait 5 minutes to allow the contents of the jars to settle, and then remove the jars very carefully with tongs. Set aside on a tea-towel for 1 hour before checking the seals (see page 161).

Avoid moving the jars for a further 12 hours (this is very important because you don't want to disturb the seal). Label and store in a cool, dark place (0–10°C); grape concentrate should keep for up to a year.

POWIDLA (POLISH PLUM BUTTER)

This Polish plum butter is made with nothing but plums. There are recipes that call for a little vanilla or cinnamon, perhaps half a cup of sugar, but I think the way forward is just plums and nothing else. It is important that the plums are very sweet, so wait as long as possible before you pick. This is a good way to use up those very ripe plums.

This plum butter is made for a good sourdough, but traditionally in Poland it is used in cakes and even added to bigos (Hunter Stew).

As the plums have to be cooked for a very long time, I think the easiest method is to make this using a slow cooker/rice cooker (you can only use a rice cooker if you have a 'warm setting'). If you don't have one of these, you'll have to do it on the stove – just be prepared to work those arm muscles (or maybe invite some friends round to help out). Apparently the word powidla *comes from the Polish* povídat, *which means to tell stories – an indication of how long it takes to get there.*

Makes 50–75ml
900g ripe plums *(traditionally the variety 'Zwetschgen' is used, also known as 'Italian Prune/Empress Plum'),* **washed, halved and destoned**
250–500ml jars suitable for heat processing *(e.g. Mason jars, see page 157); if you can get hold of smaller jars (Bormioli Rocco Quattro Stagioni) do,* **as this spread needs to be used up when opened**

Place the plums in a slow/rice cooker or a large preserving pan and cook until they have reduced to a thick mixture that sticks to the back of a wooden spoon (or doesn't drip off). This takes around 12 hours in my rice cooker with the lid propped open on warm mode. Towards the end, I switch over to the cook (rather than warm) mode and bring it to a rolling boil so that it is hot enough when it goes into the jar. This is called hot

processing and makes for a better seal. It is very important that the spread is piping hot when it goes into the jars because there is no added sugar in this recipe; you are truly relying on heat to keep this one safe.

If you find that it is not reducing enough in a preserving pan, you can bake the jam in the oven for several hours. Preheat the oven to 140°C/gas mark 2 and place the stewed plums in a large, deep baking dish. Cook for several hours, stirring occasionally, until the mixture is dark and thick.

While the plums are finishing off, fill your waterbath. Fill your sterilised jars with warm water, put them in the waterbath and boil rapidly for 10 minutes on a rolling boil. Place the lids and bands/seals in a separate saucepan. Your plum butter needs to go into the jars hot, so if necessary transfer to a pot and bring quickly and briefly to the boil. Carefully lift the hot jars from the waterbath, empty out the water into the saucepan containing the lids and bands to sterilise them, and place the jars on a clean tea-towel.

Fill the hot jars with the plum butter, leaving 1cm headroom (see page 161). Wipe the rims of the jars with a damp tea-towel, fish out the flat lids from the saucepan and fit them centrally on top. Put on the rings and tighten them so they are finger tight (no more or you'll never get them off again). Return the jars to the waterbath, making sure they are totally submerged, and process at a rolling boil for 20 minutes.

Take the lid off the waterbath, wait 5 minutes to allow the contents of the jars to settle, and then remove the jars very carefully with tongs. Set aside on a tea-towel for 1 hour before checking the seals (see page 161).

Avoid moving the jars for a further 12 hours (this is very important because you don't want to disturb the seals). Label and store in a cool, dark place (0–10°C); this butter should keep for up to a year.

GRAPE JELLY WITH NO SUGAR

750ml grape juice (see page 165)
I jar homemade pectin or agar agar
  flakes (following manufacturer's
  instructions) see page 130
Sugar, agave syrup or honey to taste
jam thermometer
250–500ml jars suitable for heat
  processing *(e.g. Mason jars, see
  page 157)*

Place the grape juice in a pan with the homemade pectin and sweetener (if using). If you want to sweeten the grape juice add 10ml honey (or sugar) for 60ml grape juice. Stir until the honey dissolves and then bring to the boil. Boil rapidly for approx. 10 minutes until set – use a jam thermometer if necessary. This jelly sets as it cools, so as long as you can get a bead to form on a wooden spoon (see flake test, page 140) you're fine. If you are using agar agar flakes, then combine the grape juice with sweetener (if using) and heat together, add the agar agar flakes and then bring to a boil for 1 minute (any longer and it will set very hard).

Meanwhile, fill your waterbath*. Fill your sterilised jars with warm water, put them in the waterbath and boil rapidly for 10 minutes on a rolling boil. Place the lids and bands/seals in a separate saucepan. Your grape jelly should go into the jars hot, so if necessary transfer to a pot and bring quickly and briefly to the boil. Carefully lift the hot jars from the waterbath, empty out the water into the saucepan containing the lids and bands to sterilise them, and place the jars on a clean tea-towel.

Fill the hot jars with the grape jelly, leaving 1cm headroom (see page 161). Wipe the rims of the jars with a damp tea-towel, fish out the flat lids from the saucepan and fit them centrally on top. Put on the rings and tighten them so they are finger tight (no more or you'll never get them off). Return the jars to the waterbath, making sure they are submerged, and process at a rolling boil for 15 minutes.

Take the lid off the waterbath, wait 5 minutes to allow the contents of the jars to settle, and then remove the jars very carefully with tongs. Set aside on a tea-towel for 1 hour before checking the seals (see page 161).

The jelly will set as it cools. Avoid moving the jars for a further 12 hours (this is very important because you don't want to disturb the seal). Label and store in a cool, dark place (0–10°C), where it should keep for up to a year.

* If you don't want to use a waterbath, this jam should be stored in the fridge where it will keep for several weeks.

BERRY JUICE CONCENTRATE FOR CORDIALS

*You can make a cordial using any number of ripe summer berries – from strawberries and blackberries to loganberries, raspberries or blueberries. I tend to make mine out of either blackcurrants, Oregon grapes (*Mahonia sp.*) or blackberries.*

> berries
> water
> granulated sugar, to taste
> 500ml to 1 litre jars suitable for heat
>   processing (see page 157)

Place the berries in a preserving pan and crush with a potato masher. Add a scant cup of water so that the berries just float and bring to the boil. Simmer gently until the berries are soft. Tip them into a jelly bag or clean, sterilised pillowcase (i.e. washed and ironed to sterilise) and strain for at least 2 hours, preferably overnight.

Return the juice to the preserving pan and simmer gently for 5 minutes; make sure it doesn't boil or it will start to set. Depending on the sweetness of your berries, you may wish to add a little sugar at this point (allow approx. 65–120g sugar per litre of juice).

Meanwhile, fill your waterbath. Fill your sterilised jars with warm water, put them in the waterbath and boil rapidly for 10 minutes on a rolling boil. Place the lids and bands/seals in a separate saucepan. Carefully lift the hot jars from the waterbath, empty out the water into the saucepan containing the lids and bands to sterilise them, and place the jars on a clean tea-towel.

Ladle the hot juice into your hot jars, leaving 5mm headroom (see page 161). Wipe the rims of the jars with a damp tea-towel, fish out the flat lids from the saucepan and fit them centrally on top. Put on the rings and tighten them so they are finger tight (no more or you'll never get them off again). Return the jars to the waterbath, making sure they are totally submerged, and process at a rolling boil for 15 minutes for both 500ml and 1 litre jars.

Take the lid off the waterbath, wait 5 minutes to allow the contents of the jars to settle, and then remove the jars very carefully with tongs. Set aside on a tea-towel for 1 hour before checking the seals (see page 161).

Avoid moving the jars for a further 12 hours (this is very important because you don't want to disturb the seal). Label and store in a cool, dark place (0–10°C); cordial should keep for up to a year.

SALSA VERDE

I love this salsa verde as it is surprisingly versatile. It can be served with chilli, on enchiladas or soft-shelled tacos, with tacos or as a sauce for roast pork. It is also good on baked potatoes with grilled cheese on top served with soured cream. And it can also be used as the base for a good spicy chicken soup.

2kg tomatillos

5 large chillies *(heat depending on your taste – traditionally Serrano chillies are used)*, chopped

1 white onion, chopped

3 garlic cloves, minced

a bunch of fresh coriander (plus stalks), very finely chopped

juice of 2 limes, approx. 150ml (or 4 tablespoons white wine vinegar)

salt, to taste

500ml jars suitable for heat processing (see page 157)

Preheat the oven to 160°C/gas mark 3. Scatter the tomatillos, chillies, onion and garlic over the base of a deep roasting tray and roast in the oven for about 30 minutes or until the tomatillos are soft and slightly charred.

While the tomatillos are in the oven, fill your waterbath. Fill your sterilised jars with warm water, put them in the waterbath and boil rapidly for 10 minutes on a rolling boil. Place the lids and bands/seals in a separate saucepan.

Remove the tomatillos from the oven and process them using a hand blender to a coarse purée with the coriander (add the coriander bit by bit to taste). This liquid will be hot, so go carefully. Pour the salsa into a preserving pan, add the lime juice/white wine vinegar and salt and bring slowly to the boil.

Meanwhile, carefully lift the hot jars from the waterbath, empty out the water into the saucepan containing the lids and bands to sterilise them, and place the jars on a clean tea-towel. Ladle the salsa into your hot jars, leaving 1cm headroom at the top (see page 161). Remove any trapped air bubbles using a sterilised chopstick, wipe the rims clean, centre the lids and adjust the seals to finger tightness (no more or you'll never get them off). Place in the waterbath, making sure they are covered with water. Bring the waterbath back to the boil and process for 15 minutes. Remove the waterbath lid, wait 5 minutes for the contents to settle, and then carefully remove the jars onto a folded tea-towel. Set aside for 1 hour before checking the seals (see page 161); do not disturb for a further 12 hours. Label and store. The salsa verde should keep for up to a year somewhere dark between 0 and 10°C.

PRESERVED ARTICHOKES

I grow eight plants, which by the height of summer usually give me 30 or more globe artichoke heads to eat. I never thought I'd say this, but there is such a thing as too many steamed chokes.

In this recipe the tender hearts of the artichoke are marinated in wine vinegar and olive oil and then waterbathed so that they are there for you in winter, when you need that taste of summer. I find one jar is enough for pizzas and so on. Once opened, store in the fridge and top up with more olive oil if necessary.

You can go about this recipe in two ways, depending on whether or not you can bear to throw away the outer leaves. If you don't want to waste all that goodness, it probably makes sense to invite some friends round when you are doing this and eat up the outer leaves with vinaigrette, leaving the hearts for preserving. The other option is to strip the outer leaves and compost them, leaving the hearts to preserve. Ideally, you'd just use baby artichokes, no bigger than an egg when on the plant. But I find I end up with a variety of sizes, so I just chop the large hearts into mouthful-sized pieces.

20 or so artichokes *(enough heads to pack a 1 litre jar)*

juice of 1 lemon

300ml white wine vinegar

250ml water

½ teaspoon black peppercorns

1 teaspoon whole coriander seeds

2 sprigs thyme, roughly chopped

2 large bay leaves

1 scant teaspoon salt

300ml olive oil

1 litre preserving jar suitable for heat processing (see page 157)

Remove all the tough outer leaves from your artichokes until you get down to the pale yellow leaves. Trim the top 2.5cm off the artichokes' hearts and cut away most of the stalks, leaving 2–3cm

remaining. Using a paring knife, peel the stalks to remove the tough outer layer (the stalks are delicious as long as they are still tender and a little flexible). Tidy up around the core of each heart, removing any green bits. To stop them going brown, drop the hearts into a pan of cold water to which you've added the lemon juice while you prepare the rest.

To cook the hearts, bring a large pan of water to the boil and cook until tender, about 10 minutes; drain.

Meanwhile fill your waterbath. Fill your sterilised jar with warm water, put it in the waterbath and boil rapidly for 10 minutes on a rolling boil. Place the lid and band/seal in a separate saucepan.

Meanwhile bring the vinegar, water, spices, herbs and salt to the boil in a separate preserving pan.

Remove the jar from the waterbath, pour the water inside the jar over the lid to sterilise it and place the jar on a tea-towel. Pack the hot jar with your hot artichoke hearts and pour over the hot vinegar solution. Top up the jar with olive oil so that the artichokes are totally submerged. (You could add the oil to the vinegar solution when you are heating it, but as the oil will separate from the vinegar in storage I think there is little to be won by doing this.) Make sure you leave a generous 2cm headroom gap at the top (see page 161).

Wipe the rim clean, centre the lid and adjust the seal to finger tightness (no more or you'll never get them off). Place in the waterbath, making sure it is totally submerged. Bring your waterbath back to the boil, set the timer and process for 25 minutes.

Remove the waterbath lid, wait 5 minutes for the contents to settle and then carefully remove the jar on to a folded tea-towel (if you find it difficult to remove the jar safely from the hot water, allow the waterbath to cool completely before removing it). Set aside for 1 hour before checking the seal (see page 161); do not disturb for a further 12 hours. Label and store somewhere out of direct sunlight between 0 and 10°C. Preserved artichokes should keep for up to a year.

If you find yourself in the enviable position of having more tomatoes than your freezer has space for, bottling your own tomato sauce is the solution. This sauce will take any size tomato, but be warned: essentially you are juicing your toms, so you need plenty for it to be worthwhile. If you just have several pounds, it may be more worthwhile to bottle them whole.

WHOLE TOMATOES WITH NO ADDED LIQUID

This recipe works best for smaller quantities of tomatoes. Note that you do have to process for over an hour to allow the heat to penetrate deep inside the toms and make them safe, so weigh up how much time you have to stand around a boiling pot of water. If you are short of time, you could crush the tomatoes in order to reduce the processing time (I would recommend doing this at the last moment of cooking to prevent the tomato pips making the sauce bitter). However, I love the sight of a jar of whole tomatoes standing on the shelf; the flavour is concentrated and as long as there's something good on the radio those extra 40 minutes don't bother me.

> ripe tomatoes – *preferably plum tomatoes that will fit nicely into your jar*
> citric acid *(or bottled lemon juice – avoid fresh lemon juice because it varies in acidity)*
> salt
> 500ml or 1 litre jars suitable for heat processing (see page 157)

Fill the waterbath and sterilise the jars by filling them with water and boiling for 10 minutes on a rolling boil; place the lids and seals in a separate pan (see page 161).

Meanwhile, skin the tomatoes. Fill a large saucepan with water and bring to the boil. Working in small batches, immerse the tomatoes in boiling water for a minute or so until the skins crack. Remove the tomatoes immediately and plunge them into a bowl of cold water. The skins should slip off easily if you apply a little pressure with your fingers. (If your toms are large fruiting varieties, you may need to remove the cores and quarter them to fit inside your jars.)

Place the tomatoes in a large saucepan and cover with water. Bring to the boil over a medium heat, stirring gently and boil for 5 mintues.

Remove your jars from the waterbath, carefully pour the hot water inside the jars over the lids/seals to sterilise them, and then place the jars on a folded towel. Before packing the jars, add a little citric acid (or lemon juice) and salt to each one. Allow ¼ teaspoon citric acid (or 1 tablespoon bottled lemon juice) and ⅓ teaspoon salt per 500ml jar. Pack the tomatoes on top, ladling hot cooking liquid into the jars to cover the tomatoes, leaving 1cm headroom (see page 161) and press down gently so that any air pockets fill up with juice. If necessary, use a sterilised chopstick to remove any air bubbles. Wipe the rims with a clean, damp cloth, centre the lids and adjust the seals to finger tightness (no more or you'll never get them off again).

Place your jars in the waterbath, making sure they are totally submerged in the water. Bring the waterbath back to a rolling boil and process for 40 minutes for 500ml jars or 1 litre jars. If you want to pack your tomatoes in commercial or homemade tomato juice you have to increase the time to 85 minutes for both 500ml and 1 litre jars. It does give a more intense flavour.

Remove the waterbath lid, wait 5 minutes for the contents to settle, and then very carefully remove the jars on to a folded tea-towel*. Check the seals after 1 hour (see page 161); do not disturb for a further 12 hours. Label and store in a cool, dark place (0–10°C) for up to a year.

* If you have a very large jar that is hard to remove safely from the hot water, allow the waterbath to cool completely before removing the jar.

BASIC TOMATO SAUCE WITH BASIL

tomatoes
citric acid *(or bottled lemon juice – avoid*
   fresh lemon juice because it varies in
   acidity)
salt
basil leaves
mouli-style food mill
500ml or 1 litre preserving jars suitable
   for heat processing (see page 157)

Fill the waterbath and sterilise your jars by filling with hot water and processing in the waterbath for 10 minutes; place the lids in a separate saucepan (see page 161).

Wash and sort the tomatoes, discarding any bruised bits, and chop into quarters. Place in a heavy-based pan and cook gently over a low heat until the tomatoes soften and break down, about 20 minutes; you might have to do this in batches. Mash with a potato masher to break the tomatoes down further and then boil until soft and juicy.

Working in batches, strain the tomatoes through a mouli-style food mill to remove the skin and pips. (These can be dried and turned into a tomato seasoning, see page 201.) The resulting liquid will be very thin, so return it to the pan and reduce by at least one-third (or until it looks more like a sauce).

Remove your jars from the waterbath, carefully pour the hot water inside the jars over the lids to sterilise them, and then place the jars on a folded tea-towel.

Pour the tomato sauce into a measuring jug and calculate the amount of citric acid (or lemon juice) and salt needed. For every 500ml sauce, allow ¼ teaspoon citric acid (or 1 tablespoon lemon juice) and ½ teaspoon salt. The sauce needs to be piping hot when it goes into the jars, so return it to the pan and bring briefly to the boil.

Using a wide-mouthed funnel, ladle the hot sauce into the hot jars so that there is 1cm headroom at the top. Add a basil leaf or two to each jar. Remove any trapped air bubbles inside the jar using a sterilised chopstick, wipe the rims clean, centre the lids and adjust the seals to finger tightness (no more or you'll never get them off again).

Place in the waterbath, making sure they are totally submerged in the water. Bring the waterbath back to a rolling boil, set your timer and process for 35 minutes for 500ml jars and 40 minutes for 1 litre jars.

Remove the waterbath lid and wait 5 minutes to allow the contents to settle*. Remove the jars on to a folded tea-towel and set aside for 1 hour before checking the seals (see page 161); do not disturb for a further 12 hours. Label your jars and store in a dark place at 0–10°C for up to a year.

* If you have a very large jar that is hard to remove safely from the hot water, allow the waterbath to cool completely before removing the jar.

ON FREEZING

There are times when to be able to freeze something is a blessing, to suspend time long enough to gather together life and take note of its flavours. Thus, when the harvest ripens too quickly or life steps in the way, the joy of this method of preserving is its speed. Not quite as you left it fresh, but good enough once thawed to be honest to itself.

Clearly the freezer is best for prepared dishes – a frozen ratatouille will always taste better than the frozen mush that is courgettes; a frozen pesto is superior to the blackened frozen leaves of basil. The home freezer is never quite clever enough to capture the essence of those store-bought peas that were frozen merely minutes after they were picked, but there are tricks to be had for a fruit or vegetable captured in its icy state.

I guess at this point I should say that, like all other storage methods, only fruit and veg harvested at its peak – that means only firm, ripe and flavoursome produce – should be chosen. Those overripe or less than perfect numbers should be used up fresh, as the freezer will hardly aid their position. However, I love to flout a rule.

I often freeze mixed batches of wild and summer strawberries in their imperfect state, particularly towards the end of the season when there are just a few here or there. In winter, when the light is utterly blue and so am I, I can quickly defrost these summer delights and whip them into something cheering. As they are in a less than perfect state, being frozen at the end of the season, they quickly defrost into rather a pale, deflated syrupy mass. However, with a little sugar and a touch of heat it is possible to reincarnate them into something close to jam to spread on warm toast, run around yogurt or spoon into porridge.

The truth is I do not love my freezer that much. I much prefer a fermented batch of beans to any frozen; I'd rather take my chance with my underground store than bank upon the freezer. There seems to be too little inherent skill in the freezer and it does not ennoble its food in any way. It does not better the game. It is, at best, a temporary solution.

Thus, I often merrily tip the good rules on their head and preserve very small batches of imperfect strawberries or save the sprouting potatoes by turning them into frozen chips, or quickly cut off the moulding bit of a butternut squash and roast and freeze the rest. I make use of its speed, its ability to save and then I hold true that like all storage products the joy here isn't to admire them for years to come, but to use them up. Eat, people, and eat up quickly!

TIPS ON FREEZING

If you are lucky enough to have space for a large chest freezer, I suggest you invest in a copy of *How to Freeze* by Carolyn Humphries. As its name suggests, it teaches you everything you need to know about freezing and freezer management (the latter being oh so important if you don't want to end up with four years' worth of redcurrants at the bottom of your drawers).

Organising your freezer

The number one rule of the freezer is to label everything. Ms Humphries suggests a hyper-organised colour-coded system with a list of contents stuck to the outside of the freezer: red for meat, green for vegetables and so on, with 'b' for bread, 's' for soup, etc. In another life, I might adopt this system, but I have no talent for such organisation. My system would remain ridiculous and whimsical. I have a 'really fishy stock for a fishy something' and 'a ratatouille that can't be beat' in my freezer at the moment. I am, however, good at putting on a date. The Sharpie is your best friend as far as the freezer is concerned.

It does make a lot of sense not to shove the latest thing on top of what came before, as this method means that the four-year-old redcurrants quickly become five. A little organisation goes a long way.

Defrosting your freezer

You should defrost your freezer every year, perhaps even twice a year. You know you should do this because the freezer door won't shut properly otherwise, which means it won't run efficiently – and all sorts of weird and not very nice bacteria will end up living in those great mounds of ice.

It makes sense to defrost the freezer when it is snowing as you can then use out of doors as your temporary freezer. It also makes sense to defrost your freezer before a great glut. These two moments rarely come together, so don't use this an excuse not to do it. However tempting it is to use a knife and hammer to pick away, don't. Hearing the fine whistle of refrigerants leaking out into the ozone is depressing and sets back all your good work on storing (and I say this from experience).

Containers

There are a few things worth saying about containers. I use a lot of recycled plastic takeaway containers and aluminium trays. You can cut up cereal boxes to make new lids, extending their life indefinitely (just make sure the coloured side of the cardboard is facing away from the food). I am increasingly uncertain about using plastic containers for storing food (even food-grade plastic, and it goes without saying that all your plastic should be food grade). I just worry about it degrading and those little bits of microscopic polymer ending up in my food. Saying that, they are useful for portion sizes. Yogurt pots and margarine tubs are both good sizes (although these days they are only really suitable for short-term storage because of the degrading problem). If the lids do not fit well, you should overwrap with foil or a plastic bag.

I also use silicone cupcake holders for freezing pesto and other sauces, as they are just the right size for two-people portions. Ice-cube trays are great for freezing portions of herbs, spinach and stock. All of these can then be stored in plastic freezer bags or aluminium foil.

It is very important to remove the air from plastic bags as this prevents oxidation. That old trick with a drinking straw is fun, but just squeezing the air out of the bag and wrapping it up tightly works just as well.

Large glass jars (the sort used for large gherkin pickles) are good for storing soups; just leave headroom for expansion.

WHAT TO FREEZE

AUBERGINES
BLANCHING TIME
3 minutes
(unpeeled, sliced into thick discs)
in water with a tablespoon
of lemon juice
12
MONTHS

FRESH BORLOTTI OR DRYING BEANS
BLANCHING TIME
3 minutes
12
MONTHS

BROAD BEANS
BLANCHING TIME
3 minutes
12
MONTHS

FRENCH BEANS
BLANCHING TIME
2 minutes
Can be sliced or chopped
12
MONTHS

RUNNER BEANS
BLANCHING TIME
2 minutes
Can be sliced or chopped
12
MONTHS

BROCCOLI
BLANCHING TIME
2 minutes
Broken into florets
12
MONTHS

CHARD
BLANCHING TIME
**Stalks 2 minutes
Leaves 1 minute**
Need to be separated
6
MONTHS

CARROTS
BLANCHING TIME
3 minutes
Sliced
12
MONTHS

CAULIFLOWER
BLANCHING TIME
3 minutes
Broken into florets
12
MONTHS

GREENS
including chard, mustards, etc.
BLANCHING TIME
1 minute
Whole leaves
6
MONTHS

KALE
BLANCHING TIME
1 minute
6
MONTHS

HERBS
No need to blanch
see page 187
6
MONTHS

HORSERADISH
No need to blanch
Mix with lemon juice or white wine
vinegar – best grated
6
MONTHS

KOHL RABI
BLANCHING TIME
2 minutes
Cut into even slices
12
MONTHS

LEEKS
BLANCHING TIME
2 minutes
Sliced
12
MONTHS

Blanching is an essential part of freezing – those brief minutes in boiling water destroy enzymes that cause deterioration, thus suspending animation.

Blanching also helps to preserve vitamin C and, to some extent, improves colour and texture. Blanching times are not estimated but scientifically

PAK CHOI
BLANCHING TIME
2 minutes

12 MONTHS

PEAS
BLANCHING TIME
1 minute

12 MONTHS

PEPPER (BELL)
BLANCHING TIME
3 minutes (whole)
1 minute (sliced)

6 MONTHS

PEPPER (CHILLI)
No need to blanch

6 MONTHS

POTATOES
BLANCHING TIME
2 minutes
Sliced into chips

12 MONTHS

RHUBARB
BLANCHING TIME
1 minute
Cut into chunks

12 MONTHS

SPRING GREENS
BLANCHING TIME
1 minute

6 MONTHS

SQUASHES, SUMMER
courgettes, spaghetti squash, etc.
BLANCHING TIME
1 minute
Best grated

12 MONTHS

SQUASHES, AUTUMN
pumpkins, etc.
Best cooked until tender

6 MONTHS

SALSIFY OR SCORZONERA
BLANCHING TIME
3 minutes
(sliced)

12 MONTHS

SPINACH
BLANCHING TIME
1 minute
Whole leaves

12 MONTHS

SPRING GREENS OR GREEN CABBAGE
BLANCHING TIME
1 minute

6 MONTHS

SWEDE
BLANCHING TIME
2 minutes
cut into even chunks

12 MONTHS

SWEETCORN
BLANCHING TIME
5 minutes
Whole

12 MONTHS

TOMATOES
No need to blanch
Store cherry tomatoes whole
or prepare as a sauce

12 MONTHS

TOMATILLO
No need to blanch,
but best frozen roasted

12 MONTHS

decided. If you choose to adjust them, even by 30 seconds, you could end up with mush. This is why it is a good idea to have a bowl of icy cold water ready to plunge your veg into, otherwise they will continue to cook as they cool down. Once cool, pat dry with a clean towel, bag, label and suck out the air.

Soft Fruit

Soft fruit such as blackberries, blueberries, strawberries, currants, figs and raspberries do not need to be blanched before storing; this would just turn them to mush. Instead, open freeze on a baking tray and once frozen store in a suitable container. This method means the berries are free flowing, otherwise you'll end up with a great lump of currants or strawberries that will thaw into a mess.

For red, white and blackcurrants or elderberries, use the back of a fork to prise off the fruit first. I don't wash the fruit first, although I do pick over for any spoils. Instead, I wash the fruit just as it starts to defrost as I find it holds its shape better this way.

All soft fruit will store for 12 months; it will take 1–2 hours to defrost.

Freezing in a heavy syrup

For some fruits, freezing in a heavy syrup saves time – particularly if you are then going to use them for pies and crumbles – and often preserves the flavour and texture better.

Traditionally, a heavy syrup is used made with two parts sugar to one part water (or 350–400g sugar for every 600ml water). I personally favour a lighter version made with 225g sugar to 600ml water, and don't always restrict myself to cane or beet sugar. Agave, maple or date syrup can all be substituted.

First blanch your fruit if necessary; this is recommended for rhubarb. Make up your sugar syrup. Place the sugar and water in a heavy-based pan and dissolve over a gentle heat. Pack your fruit into a freezerproof container and top up with sugar syrup. Remember to leave 1cm or so headroom before putting on the lid to allow for expansion in the freezer. Stored in sugar syrup, your fruit should keep for 12 months.

Freezing herbs

Many herbs don't store very well in the freezer and lose their looks quickly. This is especially true of basil leaves, which quickly turn to a black mush.

However, some herbs can be frozen successfully. Parsley, sage, thyme and rosemary all keep fairly well in the freezer and will store for up to 6 months. For these herbs, simply strip away any hard stalks but keep the leaves whole (parsley has flavoursome stalks, so you can leave these on.) Pack into freezer bags, suck out the air and seal. To use, merely crumble the frozen leaves (and stalks) into your dish.

For soft-leaf herbs such as coriander, basil, chervil, mint, coriander and savory, a better approach is to finely chop the herbs first and preserve them in oil. Not only does this method keep their brilliant colour, but it is convenient for cooking because it cuts down on preparation time and you can make medleys of flavours for specific dishes. To make individual portions of finely chopped herbs, place the chopped herbs in ice-cube trays and top up with olive oil. Once they are set, you can decant them into freezer bags, suck out the air and label. The storage time is 6 months.

Freezing juice

Small amounts of fruit juice freeze very well. Sometimes it is necessary to heat the fruit slightly to release its juices. Or you could use a juice extractor. It is worthwhile straining through a jelly bag (particularly for soft berry or cherry juices). You can either store it unsweetened or sweeten with 65–120g sugar per 1 litre of juice. Pour into containers leaving enough headroom to allow for expansion in the freezer, and then seal and freeze.

Freezing raw beans

I often keep a bag of blanched beans in my freezer for last-minute meals. They are a great way of bulking out soups and stews. The advantage of blanching them first is it cuts down on the cooking time later, making them a great fallback when you don't have the energy or time for an overnight soak. This method works for raw borlotti beans and other drying beans such as black turtle, orca and pea beans.

Shell the beans and blanch briefly in boiling water for 3 minutes. Drain, refresh under cold water and spread out on a tea-towel to dry. Scatter the beans over a baking sheet or similar and open freeze until frozen. Tip into a freezer bag, suck out the air and seal. Store for up to 12 months.

HOMEMADE CHIPS

I rarely use my best potatoes for these, but rather use this method to rescue those potatoes that won't store because they are damaged or are starting to sprout, which means, yes, I am the sort that rubs a sprout off.

I own a wonderful vintage chipper that I picked up on eBay; otherwise, you'll have to cut by hand.

> **potatoes**
> **olive oil**
> **salt**

Peel your potatoes if you wish; your decision will probably depend on the condition of your potatoes. Cut into chip shapes and parboil in boiling water for 2 minutes; drain and cool quickly.

Divide your chips between freezer bags, add a glug of oil and a good pinch of salt and toss them around to coat them evenly. (The oil will stop them sticking together and make your portions easier to remove from the freezer later.) Seal the bag and suck out the air. Store in the freezer for up to 3 months (by which point you should be back into new potatoes).

To cook your chips, preheat the oven to 200°C/gas mark 6. Scatter the chips over a baking tray and bake in the oven until golden brown, approx. 20 minutes. I never fry as I don't own a fryer and I never thaw first.

PURÉED VEGETABLES

I mainly use this technique for storing vegetables that have become spoiled but are salvageable. Pumpkins beginning to mould, carrots with carrot fly – essentially where I can chop out the bad and save the good. Puréed vegetables work brilliantly in soups and risottos when time is short.

Preheat your oven to 180°C/gas mark 4. Peel your vegetables if necessary and cut into rough chunks. Spread them out on a roasting tray, drizzle with olive oil, pop in a garlic clove or two and roast in the oven until tender. (Alternatively, boil until tender.) Transfer the cooked vegetables to a food-processor and process to a purée (or mash with a potato masher).

Store in suitable portion sizes in a rigid container, leaving a centimetre or so headroom to allow for expansion. Stored this way, your purée should last for up to 12 months.

PASSATA

If you don't have time to bottle, this is one of the best ways to store your glut of tomatoes. My favourite freezer find is a bag of this passata. It is very versatile and can be used wherever a recipe calls for a tin of tomatoes.

As an alternative to tomatoes, you could use tomatillos, but I would stick to garlic, oil and lime juice as a flavouring. The resulting sauce makes a fine base for a Mexican spicy soup or can be eaten with pork or chicken, much like you might use a salsa.

roughly 500g tomatoes, ripe, semi-ripe or
    even green; quarter large ones,
    cherries can be left whole
a couple of garlic cloves, left whole
sprig of rosemary
a small handful of oregano
salt and brown sugar, to taste
½ teaspoon coriander seeds or dried
    chillies (optional)
olive oil

Preheat the oven to 180°C/gas mark 4. Scatter your tomatoes over the base of a roasting tin and put in the garlic cloves, rosemary, oregano and a pinch or two of salt and brown sugar. Sprinkle some coriander seeds or chilli, if you wish. Pour over a glug of good olive oil and roast in the oven until bubbling and golden. Set aside to cool.

You can either freeze the roasted tomatoes as they are by putting them straight into a container, or you can blend or process them into a smooth sauce. Either way, you need to remove the garlic skins (although I have been known to blend them with little ill effect!). Store in an airtight container or freezer bag in the freezer for up to 12 months.

Enjoy as a true flavour of late summer, either in soups or sauces. To serve as a pasta sauce, simply thaw and reheat for 6 minutes or so. Whole roasted tomatoes can be served on top of baked fish or alongside polenta.

BROAD BEAN AND CHICKPEA FALAFELS

If you run into a glut of broad beans then I can't think of a better way to use them up than falafels. Stored in the freezer, along with some pitta bread, they are a simple, nourishing last-minute supper, perfect for after the pub (if you remember to take them out of the freezer before you go out).

Makes 32 small falafels

500g broad beans (or a mixture of cooked chickpeas and broad beans)

1 garlic clove *(more if you like but remember it will to all intents and purposes be raw)*

1 small onion, peeled and diced

1 small dried chilli, crushed

a small handful flat-leaf parsley (stems and all)

a small handful dill

a small handful mint

1 tablespoon coriander seeds *(I used fresh seed from the garden)* or a small handful fresh coriander leaf

2 teaspoons cumin seeds

1 tablespoon sesame seeds

1 teaspoon baking powder

olive oil

salt and pepper, to taste

flour, for dusting

Blanch the broad beans for 3 minutes (if they are rather large and a bit tough remove their skins). If you don't have enough broad beans then, use half broad beans and half chickpeas. In a bowl combine broad beans, chickpeas, herbs, spices and baking powder and, using a hand blender or food-processor, start to blend the mixture together. Add just a touch of olive oil as you go to keep the mixture moving. You want a sausage meat-like consistency, but aim for the dry side.

Taste the mixture and season as necessary.

If the mixture feels too wet to roll into balls, then add a little flour or, if you have any to hand, breadcrumbs. Rub a little olive oil into the palm of your hands and roll the mixture into small balls, about 5cm or so. Dust in a little more flour and set aside.

Fry in oil in a wok or deep frying pan for 20-30 seconds or until golden brown.

Serve with minted yogurt (just mint and yogurt) or tahini.

To freeze, lay the uncooked falafels on parchment paper and open freeze (this will stop them sticking together). Once they have frozen, you can pack them into bags, remove the air, seal and label. Stored like this, they will keep in the freezer for up to 6 months.

To reheat, arrange the falafels on a baking sheet in a single layer and allow to defrost. Fry in hot oil until golden brown on both sides. Drain on kitchen paper and serve hot on a toasted pitta bread.

PESTO MADE WITH GREENS AND HERBS

Pestos are a simple way to store herbs and leafy greens. For a basic recipe, process garlic, shelled nuts such as pine or almonds (the latter are cheaper and have a milder flavour), lemon juice and salt with any number of greens – cabbage cores, fennel or carrot fronds, basil leaves, parsley or wild garlic (in which case don't add any extra garlic) – whatever you have to hand. Traditionally, hard cheese such as Parmesan or Grano Padano is added, but I find it best to leave this out if I'm making a batch for the freezer, preferring to add it to the dish once defrosted. For pistou (a traditional French sauce served with minestrone-style soup), omit the cheese.

- a handful of pine nuts *(or shelled almonds, pumpkin or sunflower seeds – these are cheaper and milder than pine nuts)*
- 50g grated Parmesan
- 4 handfuls of greens of your choice – *kale, spinach, fennel tops, carrot fronds, etc, roughly chopped; if you are using any woody stems or cores, cook these first until tender*
- 1–2 garlic cloves, peeled and crushed
- a pinch of chopped fresh red chilli (optional)
- 4 tablespoons olive oil
- 2 tablespoons lemon juice *(that's roughly half a small lemon)*
- salt, to taste

Toast the nuts in the oven at 140°C/ gas mark 2 for 5 minutes; basically you have to keep an eye on them so that they don't burn as this can happen easily.

Place the nuts, Parmesan, kale, garlic, chilli, olive oil and lemon juice in a food processor and blend. Taste and season as necessary. At this point you can add more greens, Parmesan, olive oil, nuts or lemon juice as you see fit.

Either serve immediately or place into a suitable freezer container, remove any air, seal and freeze. It will store for 6 months.

EATING TOP
TO TAIL

It becomes imperative not to waste a single bit of your vegetables not out of parsimony but because that which we discard can sometimes be the best bits of a cook's repertoire. Odd cuts of meat are having a huge renaissance. Offal, liver, kidneys and the like have all become trendy again, with every hip restaurant in the land championing head-to-tail eating. I suppose it is not surprising that vegetables have been left out; people have a hard enough time eating enough of the pretty bits. However, I for one am going to stand up for the roots, stems and sprouts so readily ignored. Add all these bits up together and there are extra meals to be had.

I'd thoroughly recommend reading *Food in England* by the late, great Dorothy Hartley. When all you've been left with after a damp and disastrous summer is potatoes, cabbages, swedes and turnips, here is a book that will make you proud of what little you did harvest. It is filled with invaluable tips for eating all that is on offer – from simmering the shredded outer leaves of a cauliflower, mid-ribs removed, in pepper, milk and bay leaves to using the non-woody part of the stem for making soup cubes.

ANY LEAF PESTO

The leafy tops of fennel, the core of a cabbage, the green tips of a turnip, even the leafy fronds of carrots are not for the compost (though this is a noble place to leave them), they are for your fridge and later your lunch and perhaps again for supper on top of pasta. I use up all manner of cabbage bits to make into pesto –the tops of Brussels sprout plants, the internal core of young cabbage (as long as it has not become woody) and any outer leaves of the cabbage tender enough to be pulsed, but too ragged to be dished up.

The joy of these green and white bits is that they hold the essence of the plant's flavour. A little simmering for the outer cabbage leaves and cores, a straight blend for say the fennel, a garlic clove or two (or more if you are dining alone), a squeeze of lemon, some almonds, walnuts or, if your budget reaches, pine nuts, a little salt, perhaps some pepper, pecorino or Parmesan and you have a fine pesto (see page 195). This pesto freezes wonderfully, but I prefer to leave out the cheese until after defrosting because I think the flavour is impaired by all that cold. I use silicone cupcake holders as storage containers, as they are the perfect amount to feed four, or use ice-cube trays for single portions. Or I just store in a jar in the fridge for tomorrow's use.

I serve this up on pasta with plenty of grated Parmesan and doused in a little more olive oil. I eat this on toast, on crackers and on baked potatoes.

CARL LEGGE'S CARROT TOP PESTO

Carl lives on the Llyn peninsula in Wales and is the author of the Permaculture Kitchen *(and he is behind many of the tips in this section). Let's just say he's a man dedicated to not wasting the good bits.*

> a large bunch of carrot tops
> 25g whole almonds or hazelnuts *(I've made it with walnuts too)*
> 1 large garlic clove, peeled and chopped
> 25g Parmesan
> 100ml olive oil
> sea salt and pepper, to taste

Wash the carrot tops and boil briefly to wilt the leaves. Strain and refresh with cold water to stop them cooking further; they should still look bright green. Squeeze out as much excess liquid as possible or you'll dilute the recipe.

Dry roast the almonds in the oven (160°C/gas mark 3 for about 10 minutes) or in a heavy-based pan, turning the almonds regularly to stop them from burning.

Blend the almonds, garlic and a small amount of the carrot leaves in a food-processor and blitz until finely chopped. Slowly add the remaining carrot leaves in batches, followed by the Parmesan and blend to a coarse purée. Slowly add the olive oil until you have a smooth consistency, tasting as you go (you may need to add more or less oil depending on how old your carrot leaves are). Season to taste and enjoy.

This pesto is good over roasted vegetables or fish. It will keep for several days in an airtight container in the fridge or can be frozen.

Coleslaw

Now some people might think coleslaw is an abomination, and that is certainly true of the stuff supermarkets produce on the cheap, but there is nothing cheap about homemade slaw. There are plenty of leftover bits you can add to your slaw to turn it into something special, including shredded broccoli cores, finely shredded cabbage or chopped up celeriac or carrots. Combine whatever you have available with three parts mayonnaise to one part grain mustard, add a little soured cream, a squeeze of lemon juice or white wine vinegar, some salt, pepper and minced parsley and serve chilled. You could add some sliced apple, capers, chopped pickled gherkins or a little minced dill if you like. This will store in the fridge for a day or two.

Eat your greens

The tougher outer leaves of cabbages and other brassicas are particularly good fried with potatoes or added to bubble and squeak – in fact, they are better than the more tender leaves because they have a bit of a bite to them. The leaves of any broccoli or purple sprouting broccoli can also be used, just as you would any other green.

Beetroot leaves are edible; they can be used just like Swiss chard. Younger leaves are less metallic tasting than older leaves, which I think are best destined for the stockpot. You can either grow beetroot specifically for its young leaves – 'Bull's Blood', with its dark, metallic leaves is good for this – or you can harvest the leaves as you harvest the roots. (Avoid harvesting the leaves across the growing season because you'll affect the size of the root, which is not a wise idea.)

To make the very best tomato sauce for pasta, add a single fresh leaf from the tomato plant (yes, a lot of them will make you sick, but a single leaf won't kill you) towards the end of cooking. This single leaf imparts something of the tomato's true aroma – that special essence of tomatoes that is so hard to capture. Remove the leaf before serving.

HERBS The soft stems of dill, coriander, parsley and basil can withstand heat better than the leaves. These can be used at the start of a dish, say fried with a little garlic. Woodier stems such as thyme and rosemary can be added to stocks. Rosemary makes for great skewers; don't use bay stalks in this way because the wood contains poison.

The roots of coriander are widely used in Thai cuisine; the flavour is distinctly of coriander, but deeper and works well in soups and stews. I like to use the roots (well washed and scrubbed) in pickles, vinaigrettes and in curries. You can freeze the roots for long-term storage.

FRUIT Freeze apple cores and peelings for making pectin (see page 130). For best results, use under-ripe fruit/green apples, which are higher in pectin.

Vegetable stockpot

The leaves of pretty much anything other than potatoes can go into your stockpot – beet leaves, celery leaves, carrots, radish, tough cabbage mid-ribs and leek leaves, the woody parts of asparagus, the stems of parsley, basil and thyme, the outer skins of onions (even the brown bits, which will dye your stock a lovely golden brown, essential for consommés and broths), and any sprouting tops of onions and garlic too. Even the scrubbed peelings of potatoes, parsnips, carrots and Jerusalem artichokes work wonderfully. Add a little salt, a little white wine if you have it to hand and a good grind of pepper and allow it to simmer over a low heat until it tastes good before straining.

I tend to add a lot of celery leaf and adjust the rest of the vegetables to taste, depending on what is available. This water is charged with good stuff; use it to reheat cooked vegetables, for cooking pasta or rice or just as the basis of tomorrow's soup.

Runner bean crostini

When you are left with a glut of runner beans that are too stringy and too fat with beans for eating alone, try blitzing the lot into a topping for crostini or a dip for tacos (in which case you might like to add some chilli to the basic recipe). Top, tail and string the beans and cook until tender in boiling water (save the cooking liquor for adding to stocks). Roughly chop the beans and transfer to a blender. Add a glug of olive oil, a couple of raw garlic cloves, some salt and pepper and a good dollop of crème fraîche or soured cream and blitz to a coarse purée. Serve warm on grilled sourdough, perhaps with a poached egg on top to make a supper of it. A similar spread can be made with slightly too large and too tough broad beans, which is wonderful with scrambled eggs on toast. Another of Carl's recipes is to make a purée of the pods. Boil them until tender, put through a mouli to remove any strings and flavour with butter, cream and a little dill or tarragon. Season to taste.

Pea pod soup

Pea pods are too tough to eat, but as Dorothy Hartley suggests they can be made into the base for a delicate soup. Place the pods in a pan, barely cover with water and simmer for an hour, covered. Pass the now softened pods through a fine sieve and use the liquor as the base for a very delicate clear pea soup. Alternatively, you can turn it into a fine summer minestrone by adding a handful of cooked brown rice, some young peas, a little shredded cabbage, some baby carrots and a sprig or two of mint.

Small broad bean pods, not much bigger than your thumb in thickness, can be treated in much the same way as pea pods.

Overcooked or undercooked vegetables

Overcooked vegetables can be turned into a perfectly good warm salad. Allow the vegetables to cool and cube (as best you can, removing any burnt bits if necessary). Dress with a warm Dijon vinaigrette or go for a Russian salad, adding cubed sour dill pickle, equal parts of soured cream and mayonnaise, a little mustard, minced dill and parsley and some salt and pepper to taste.

Undercooked vegetables can be briefly roasted or grilled with olive oil, rosemary and a little garlic until golden brown. Serve these mixed with lettuce in a warm salad, perhaps with some chorizo or cured meat.

Dried tomato skin seasoning

I've adapted this idea from Liana Krissoff's *Canning for a New Generation*. In it she suggests making a dried tomato peel powder for garnishing any number of dishes. I generally don't have enough tomatoes to make a straight powder, so I have adapted her recipe into a seasoning.

This recipe is a satisfying way of using up all those tomato skins left over from bottling (see page 175). Spread the skins out over a baking sheet lined with parchment paper and leave to dry on a sunny windowsill (or bake in the oven or dehydrator for 1 hour at 80°C). Once dry, blitz in a herb grinder with some salt, dried chillies and a little dried oregano. This is the perfect condiment for eggs of any sort or just use as a sweet, spicy salt for the table.

CALENDAR FOR PRESERVING

January, February, March

Cabbages, winter greens, such as purple sprouting broccoli, mustards	Sauerkraut, Gundruk, cold store, in ground storage
Winter radishes, turnips	Pickle, cold store, in ground storage in mild areas (protect with fleece)
Marrows, pumpkins	Frost-free storage (10°C), jam, chutney, ferment, freeze
Parsnips, carrots	In-ground storage, cold store in sand, pickle, freeze
Potatoes	Cold store, freeze
Culinary herbs	Dry, freeze, preserve in salt (parsley)

April, May

Rhubarb	Bottle, jam, freeze

June

Gooseberries, strawberries	Bottle, jam, freeze, dry
Culinary herbs	Dry in salt, freeze
Baby beetroots	Pickle, chutney

July

Blackcurrants, berries, redcurrants, rhubarb, strawberries	Bottle, jam, chutney, freeze, dry (whole or as fruit leather)
Culinary herbs	Dry, freeze, preserve in salt
Peas	Freeze
Shallots	Dry, pickle
Fennel	Pickle

August

Tomatoes	Bottle, dry, freeze, chutney, jam, cold store, freeze juice
Apples	Bottle, jam, chutney, cordial
Plums, blackberries	Jam, cordial
Cucumbers	Ferment, pickle
Radishes, beetroot, turnips, carrots	Ferment, pickle, cold store

Fennel	Pickle
Beans	Pickle
Courgettes	Ferment, freeze
Marrows	Store at 10°C, jam, chutney
Onions	Dry and store above 10°C
Cauliflower	Cold store (for up to 10 days), pickle

September

Apples	Cold store, dry, jam, chutney, freeze juice
Tomatoes, tomatillos, chillies	Bottle, dry, freeze, pickle, ferment (chillies only)
Beetroot, turnips, swedes, carrots	Cold store, pickle, ferment
Pears	Dry, cold store, freeze juice
Plums, damsons	Dry, jam, bottle, cordial, freeze juice
Cauliflower	Cold store (for 10 days), pickle, freeze

October

| Quinces | Jam, juice, cold store |

November

| Medlars | Jelly, cold store |

December

Apples	Cold store, dry, juice, jam, chutney
Parsnips	In-ground storage, cold store
Brussels sprouts	In-ground storage, cold store, freeze
Cabbages	Ferment, cold store
Carrots	Cold store, pickle, ferment
Celeriac	Cold store
Winter greens	Ferment, freeze, dry, pickle
Beetroot	Cold store, pickle
Potatoes	Cold store, freeze

INDEX

RESOURCE BOOK

Equipment

Jam jars

MY WECK JARS (for water bathing/canning) are all sourced from Amazon (amazon.co.uk), where you can pick up replacement clips and new rubber seals in bulk.

THE JAM JAR SHOP (jamjarshop.com) is great for bulk buys of standard jam jars, including Le Parfait.

THE PRESERVE SHOP (preserveshop.co.uk) sell Mason Jars (similar to Ball Jars from the States, suitable for waterbathing), Kilner Jars (also suitable for water bathing) and an array of pretty shaped jam jars to adorn your selves. It also sells jam making kits including maslin pans, funnels and jar covers.

REPLACEMENT RUBBER SEALS for Mason, Ball or Kilners clip jars as well as replacement metal lids for screw top jars are best sourced off Amazon for best prices.

If you find old kilner jars at flea sale, there's a man who can restore them back to safe use (preservingjarparts.co.uk).

LAKELANDS (lakeland.co.uk) is good for all sorts of home preserving and kitchen goodies.

Dehydrators

My dehydrator is a Stockli, that has served me well, but the prince of machines is an Excalibur dehydrator. The best prices for both are on Amazon.

Waterbath

Tala do an excellent canning equipment set for water bathing/jam making called the Tala Jam Canning Set (tongs, jar lifts, wide mouth funnels, lid lifters etc) sold on Amazon.

Kilner Jars sell a Kilner Pan Rack Trivet, which will act as a false bottom to turn any large pan (20cm diameter plus) in a water bath.

Be wary of buying any canning starter sets sold with enamel pots (or kettles for water bathing) as these will most likely come from the States/Canada and you will pay hefty import tax and shipping.

Fermenting

Gartopf fermenting pots in 5 or 10 litres, with lid, gutter and stones to weigh down your ferments, are fantastic for large scale fermenting. The best prices are on Amazon.

Websites

THE NATIONAL CENTRE FOR HOME FOOD PRESERVATION (USA)
nchfp.uga.edu
A one-stop shop for the current practices on food preservation. These people have tested everything, if they say boil for five minutes or rest for 20 then do EXACTLY that.

BALL'S FRESH PRESERVING
Freshpreserving.com
From the makers of USA Ball jars – some of the recipes are duff, others are great, but a good place to pick up tips on water bathing.

THE PICKLE BIBLIOGRAPHY
http://ncsu.edu/foodscience/USDAARS/html/Fflbiblio1.htm
For the academic pickling nerd – links to peer-reviewed papers on pickles – really!

This edition published in 2016 by Kyle Books, an imprint of Kyle Cathie Ltd.
192–198 Vauxhall Bridge Road
London SW1V 1DX
general.enquiries@kylebooks.com
www.kylebooks.co.uk

First published in 2013

ISBN: 978-0-85783-376-1
10 9 8 7 6 5 4 3 2 1

Alys Fowler is hereby identified as the author of this work in accordance with section 77 of Copyright, Designs and Patents Act 1988.

Text copyright © 2013 Alys Fowler
Photography copyright © 2013 Simon Wheeler
Design copyright © 2013 Kyle Books

Photography: Simon Wheeler
Design: Lawrence Morton
Project editor: Sophie Allen
Editorial assistant: Tara O'Sullivan
Copy editor: Catherine Ward
Production: Lisa Pinnell

A CIP record for this title is available from the British Library.

Colour reproduction by ALTA London
Printed and bound in China by 1010 Printing International Ltd.

Thanks first to Sophie Allen, my editor. In case no-one has told you recently, you rock! And to Kyle for continuing to support my funny life. To Lawrence for making this book beautiful, for which I am truly grateful. As for Simon Wheeler, I love your work (and I quite like you).

Thanks to Trudi Kerr for a wonderful afternoon learning about traditional preserving methods and to Carl Legge for his creative recipe tips. Likewise, to Birgit for plum inspiration. Clare, Emily, Sue and Les, Syd and Beth, Ingrid and Jeremy have all tasted, offered up ideas, ingredients and kitchen cheer, thank you all. Vicky Casstles not only lets me plunder her damson tree every year, but also came up top trumps when I needed a damson cheese to photograph, so thanks there, too.

Thompson and Morgan saved me when the slugs ate my seedling aubergines, thanks to Paul for a swift delivery of a new batch.

To the fermenting king and queen, Sandor Katz and Daphne Lambert for their dedication to this dark art.

But mostly, as always, to H.

Nigel Slater's recipe for baked eggs, taleggio and chutney is found in the *Marie Claire Cookbook*, published by Mitchell Beazley, 1993

Sam and Sam Clarks' preserved lemons comes from *Casa Moro*, published by Ebury Press, 2004

Sandor Katz's root kimchi comes from *Wild Fermentation* published by Chelsea Green Publications, 2003

Bibliography: see left